D0531966

20 Saying of Herman Melville

Resurrecting A E S O P

fables lawyers should remember

Also by Mike Papantonio:

IN SEARCH OF ATTICUS FINCH
A Motivational Book for Lawyers

and

CLARENCE DARROW, THE JOURNEYMAN
Lessons for the Modern Lawyer

$\mathcal{R}$esurrecting A E S O P

fables lawyers should remember

Mike Papantonio

A Seville Square Book

A Seville Square Book

Seville Publishing

Correspondence:
Post Office Box 12042
Pensacola, FL 32590

Offices:
316 South Baylen Street
Fourth Floor
Pensacola, FL 32501

Resurrecting Aesop:
Fables Lawyers Should Remember

First Seville Square Edition, April 2000
Cover Design and Illustrations: Cynthia Turner
ISBN: 0-9649711-2-7

Seville Square Books may be obtained for
educational, seminar, or promotional use in bulk quantities
at discount rates. For information, please write to:

Promotional Department
Seville Publishing Co., Inc.
Post Office Box 12308
Pensacola, Florida 32581
www.sevillepublishing.com

Child of mine . . .
As you sift through all the choices
you will need to make in your lifetime,
I hope at least one choice
is made easier by something
you have read in this book.

❧

Acknowledgments

Terri Tait Papantonio
Mary Elizabeth Cole
Diana Bailey
John Morgan
John Bray
Cynthia Turner
Herb Sadler
Fred Levin
Honorable James Haley
Charles Josey
Suzanne Barnhill
Bryan Aylstock
Justin Witkin
Tom Malone
Steve Echsner
Katie Monroe

❧

Foreword
by Robert F. Kennedy, Jr.

I N LAW, AS IN LIFE, we are challenged to walk with one foot in the spiritual realm and one in the material. As lawyers, we struggle to live by the values that bring happiness and keep us centered with God while embracing the tactics that bring us success in our professional endeavors. Mike Papantonio teaches that these ought not to be contradictory purposes.

In becoming great lawyers, we sometimes risk losing sight of the things that make us good human beings. Our work can become an addiction that robs our families and deprives us of the balance that is the emblem of a truly rich life. Job stress, high stakes, and the professional duty to vigorously defend our clients occasionally incline us toward incivility or worse. Every lawyer has the opportunity to tweak the truth, to spin a tale, or to massage the facts to gain advantage in litigation. The very gifts for justification and rationalization that make us effective lawyers may tend to decalibrate our moral compass or hobble us in our more important relationships. The moral challenges are always greatest in the hurly-burly of trial work when decisions must be made instantaneously and the perils of losing seem most frightening. Self-will often leads good lawyers into bad habits, tantalizing them with the illusory rewards of large fees, easy victories and hasty advancement.

Such choices place peace of mind, self-esteem, and reputations—those things with true spiritual value—in jeopardy. When that happens, we have got to go back to basics. Every day we must struggle to again submit self-will to God's will, a struggle with drama, difficulties, and pitfalls that are amplified by professional success. If our profession is to enhance our personal growth we must operate by the premise that there is no case and no cause that is important enough to make us compromise our basic values and no material acquisition to substitute for a virtuous life. We must constantly readjust and check our moral compass and continuously ask ourselves, "Am I doing the right thing now?" As we accumulate power and wealth that beckon us to live by our own rules, we must persistently discipline ourselves to live by the rules we learned in grade school: don't lie, cheat, or steal, and do unto others as you would have them do unto you. These are the values that place God over self and community over self-indulgence.

Mike has traced those values back even further than grade school to 600 years before Christ when the pagan philosopher, Aesop, used animal stories to teach the ancient kings of Asia Minor the same lessons in rectitude and service that I learned from the nuns in third-grade catechism. He taught them the basic tenets of eternal wisdom.

Wisdom is the knowledge of God's will. It is universal truth. Aesop's lessons transcend the barriers of religion, language, culture, geography, and time. They are as true and relevant for lawyers in twenty-first century New York as they were for the pagan royalty of Asia Minor in the sixth century B.C. Aesop's animals invariably suffer for their acts of pride, greed, self-indulgence, and obsessive ambition. They are rewarded when their conduct demonstrates the virtues of humility, integrity, kindness and commitment to community.

Law is the essence of community. The highest function of law is to foster community and to promote the development and enforcement of rules that safeguard the public from the excesses of power. Law fosters fairness and dependability in human intercourse and promotes justice and access to power for every member of the community. At our best, lawyers shield communities from the seduction of the notion that we can advance ourselves by leaving our poorer brothers and sisters behind or by trampling on the rights of the poor or future generations. Law, at its best, is a calling that asks us to transcend self-interest and spend our lives in service to community.

But law is also a path to power, money, and assets that offer the practitioner opportunity for corruption and abuse. Even the most virtuous attorney may sometimes get distracted by pride or ambition for the top of the heap. Aesop warns that that spot is usually nothing but a high place from which to tumble. Aesop's man who stares at the stars and falls in a hole reenacts a theme common to many of the philosopher's stories. Aesop understood that life, for most of us, is a struggle between self-will and God's will, between ego indulgence and community service. Like the frog who seeks to inflate himself above his fellows—until he explodes—ambition and self-indulgence often end in destruction. The lawyer who lies or bamboozles for a client, in the hope of acquiring money, fame, or power will find he's become not the king of the heap but, in Mike's apt description, "a pathetic, boorish lapdog to the highest bidder."

If we focus on professional success as the measure of ourselves, our work will devolve into ceaseless activity without personal or spiritual progress. Mike shows how the focus on self leads us to exhaust ourselves in struggles without meaning or purpose. Peace of mind, personal growth, and self-esteem come not by self-indulgence but by doing estimable things. That often means resisting the impulse for easy victory and taking the more difficult path. Real success, in the form of personal fulfillment, is achieved when we take our eyes off the horizon of pride and personal ambition and focus instead on methodically performing the little tasks of civility and service. This is the lesson that the tortoise taught the hare.

This does not mean the lawyer should abandon healthy ambition. Healthy ambition does not lead an individual to lie, cheat, or bamboozle for a client. Healthy ambition is the desire to do God's will and enjoy his blessings. Mike's conclusions confirm my own experience: good behavior often brings good fortune—either from providence, from reciprocal altruism, or from the good will and trust that we gain among our fellows. There is, of course, no guarantee that mere rectitude will bring us legal victories or prosperity. But even if it doesn't, we will still enjoy our reputation. The reputation for trustworthiness, good judgment, rectitude, and discretion, the example of a life well lived, and the invaluable respect of our peers all exceed in value the illusory victories of money and fame.

Mike asks us to listen anew to Aesop's advice that we wear life like a loose coat and cling to nothing material; the easy choices do not usually give us the benefits we expected. If we ignore the call for service to God and community in favor of material success, we risk the fate of the country mouse who discovers that the material luxury of the city comes with the danger of a big hungry cat.

The Cliffs of Delphi, where Aesop met his death.

Introduction

I N THE COURSE OF OUR LIVES, most of us have on occasion been advised to "get back to the basics." That advice may have been delivered by a coach who wanted to help us improve the way we hit a ball or swam the length of a pool. We might have heard that advice from a teacher or a college or law professor trying to help us learn a completely new twist on a subject we believed we comfortably understood. That teacher might have shown us that, to unlock the door to new ways of thinking about old subject matter, we first had to again get our mind around the very basic building blocks of that subject matter. We have been advised to "get back to the basics" by people with whom we have our closest relationships: our immediate family, our dearest friends. They have suggested to us, or we to them, that it is time to get back to the basics of what we have spent a lifetime trying to understand about quality living.

Sometime before 600 B.C., a freed slave named Aesop acquired the reputation of being a respected storyteller and philosopher who fashioned most of his philosophy and spun most of his stories around what we might refer to today as "the basics."

Not much is known about the details of Aesop's life. Historians believe that he was, late in life, a storyteller and counselor for a king's court somewhere in Asia Minor.

Historians are not able to tell us how much Aesop actually borrowed from the great teachers, thinkers, and philosophers who preceded him. But by designing parable-like short stories about relationships among dogs, wolves, geese, donkeys, and occasionally people, Aesop reconsidered and reinvented the wisdom of Homer, Solomon, Isaiah, and David, who had discussed "the basics" centuries before him.

It is clear that Aesop did not believe that most of us needed in-depth instruction about improving the quality of our lives. He assumed that most of the people hearing his fables had already heard and had already accepted and rejected his ideas thousands of times before they came across his fables.

Aesop's vehicle for reminding us about those basics does not rely on the lengthy and convoluted dialogue that was so often used by Greek philosophers. Five- or six-paragraph "reminders" were all that Aesop typically devoted to even his most profound ideas about how we should live those basics. It is clear that he believed mankind could benefit from studying the rewards and the misfortunes of the dogs, cats, lions, foxes, donkeys, and goats who had lived before us. For example, here is Aesop's fable of the Lion, the Fox, and the Donkey:

There was once a threesome hunting for food. The threesome was made up of a lion, a fox, and a donkey.

After they had hunted and gathered enough food, the donkey volunteered to divide it within the group. In fact, he divided it into almost perfectly equal shares. However, the lion expected his share to be the greatest, so, in anger, he killed the donkey and asked the fox to divide the shares. The sly fox piled the food into one huge pile and kept for himself only two tiny pieces of the freshly killed game.

The lion, who was very pleased with the distribution, asked the fox how he had learned to divide shares among friends with such fairness.

As he cautiously backed away from the lion with his two small pieces of game, the fox explained that he had learned most of what he knew about the subject matter from watching his dear friend the donkey.

Aesop, in his typical way, was advising his listeners that if we pay attention, we can learn from the good and bad choices that have already been made by other people.

This book will resurrect the lessons of Aesop. It will borrow from the wisdom of Aesop's fox. The goal of this book is to do what the fox did when he was confronted with the problem of saving his own life after he observed the unpleasant end to the life of this friend, the donkey. It is likely that Aesop was right when he told us that the secret to life is that there are no secrets any more if we pay attention to what those who have gone before us have already learned.

It is a mistake to believe that Aesop's primary goal was to try to influence the thinking of the average citizen with his commonsense basics for living. Kings and kings' courts were typically the foremost patrons of learning: kings relied on the great sages and philosophers

for education and insight about how to hold kingdoms together. Kings and their advisors were typically the audience for sages such as Aesop. The theories of good leadership—the theories about basic principles that make life more rewarding and manageable for leaders and the people they must lead—usually were developed and restated by talented thinkers such as Aesop.

The leaders Aesop was educating and enlightening around Asia Minor in the sixth century B.C. were faced with the same types of responsibilities that burden those people who have assumed a leadership role in 2000 A.D. During the time that Aesop was advising world leaders, however, those leaders were typically born to that position of responsibility. Rarely did they have the option to refuse that leadership mantle. Their responsibility to hold their culture together was a responsibility that passed through blood lines.

Fortunately, bloodlines don't create leaders in twenty-first century America. The responsibility of leadership in America is distributed among many segments of our society. Like it or not, one segment of society that has been given an inordinately large share of the responsibility to lead is that part of the American population holding J.D. degrees. Our worst critics can rant and rave about how lawyers will be the demise of the world's greatest democracy. Jay Leno, one of the funniest fat men on television, can vilify lawyers night after night. Congressmen and state legislators can continue to try to legislate us out of business. But most Americans are still counting on us to lead.

It is true that if you polled most Americans about the level of trust, respect, and admiration they have for lawyers as a faceless, nameless group, they would rank us slightly below paparazzi and slightly above politicians. What most pollsters don't tell us, however, is that when they ask those same people what they think about a specific lawyer—their personal lawyer that they rely on for advice and help or a lawyer they know personally or one who lives in their neighborhood—when those same people are asked about that lawyer with a name and a face, those same people do have respect, even admiration, for that lawyer.

Again, like it or not, and in spite of our detractors' best efforts, communities all over America are still looking to us to lead.

America is made up of thousands of small communities—tiny communities that are subparts of states, smaller than cities, tinier even than boroughs or townships. We call them neighborhoods.

Jack Kerouac and Thomas Wolfe have told some of the most important stories ever written about Americans by exploring the significance of the neighborhood in American culture. These writers recognized that the tiniest of America's geographic subdivisions, "neighborhoods," provided the building blocks for our entire culture.

Most neighborhoods obviously are bigger in 2000 than they were when Kerouac wrote *The Town and the City* or when Thomas Wolfe wrote *Look Homeward, Angel,* but not much has changed about neighborhood culture in the decades since those stories were written. If you walk to your front door, open that door, look straight ahead, look left down the street, look right up the street, you will see the building block for America's democratic culture. You will recognize that you are standing in the middle of a community democracy that is joined at the hip with our entire republic.

You will notice that you are an important building block in that republic.

This book will explore how well 800,000 of us, in our separate neighborhoods, are succeeding in understanding and living some of those basics that Aesop believed were so important for the leaders of his small world to grasp. It will reconsider some of the reminders he left for us in the context of living as a lawyer.

Aesop's task of enlightening the leadership of 600 B.C. was somewhat easier because the circle of people who guided and influenced Aesop's society was a small one. He only had to convince a relatively small group of leaders that there are some basics that we can learn that will improve our lives in predictable, sustainable ways. He only had to convince a tiny group of leaders that in order to improve the lives of everyone in their community, they first had to improve their own lives.

Perhaps Aesop was wise enough to understand that he could not change his entire contemporary world with his simple philosophy about basic principles for leadership and living. Maybe he understood that, as he told his animal stories, the best he could hope for was positive change in his small kingdom, in his neighborhood culture. It is possible that he believed that positive change in the leadership of his small subdivision of the world would eventually translate to bigger, sustainable positive changes for the world beyond his king's court.

In the time it takes you to read this book, there will be lawyers doing their damnedest to obliterate all traces of the dignity and honor that for the better part of two centuries were identified with lawyering.

Some of those lawyers simply can't help themselves because they never heard anything resembling Aesop's wisdom. Others heard and were taught the basics for better living long before they enrolled in law school, but at some point the "real business" of lawyering, in their mind, caused those basics to become less relevant. They began believing that what is not useful in their world of business is also not useful in the other parts of their lives.

And still, there is another small group within our 800,000 brother and sister J.D.'s who can best be described by the following fable:

A raven that had feathers blacker than coal
had a favorite drinking hole. At that drinking

hole lived a beautiful swan that had feathers whiter than freshly fallen snow. The black raven wanted desperately to have beautiful white feathers like the swan, so he tried to change a few of his habits. He ate the same food the swan ate, made the same noises the beautiful swan made. He dunked his head under the water every time the swan dunked his head. He washed and scrubbed his black feathers day in and day out, but his color never changed from jet black to snow white simply from his acting like the beautiful swan.

Aesop assigned this lesson to the fable of the raven and the swan: Sometimes our true nature simply cannot be changed.

Every profession has its ravens. They can dress in the finest clothes, surround themselves with all the trappings of accomplishment, gain access to all the right positions of influence, but in the end they are still ravens, not swans.

Two or three of Aesop's fables acknowledge that an awful lot of people, including lawyers, will never understand or appreciate his vision of leadership and better-quality living. Like the raven, they will routinely focus on form without much meaningful understanding about substance. Some of those people may hold titles of leadership in our world of lawyering. They may be regarded as the wealthiest, most powerful people in our profession. But those appearances won't change the fact that they are ravens, not swans.

Fortunately, the overwhelming majority of lawyers have nothing in common with Aesop's raven. They are men and women who are endlessly providing a positive impact in small community democracies throughout this country. They are the lawyers with faces and names who are respected and, yes, even admired by the people who live up and down the streets of their neighborhoods.

They are lawyers who believe that, as they take from their community, they must also give back through leadership.

This book has been written for those lawyers. It has been written as a reminder that Aesop did not write his fables with the belief that they would be understood and appreciated as sound advice for everyone. This book, hopefully, is a reminder that Aesop's fables certainly were not written for children. The truth is, most children need far fewer reminders about the basics for better living than many lawyers who have been blessed with the honor and responsibility of showing leadership and maybe even advancing and improving the quality of their own community democracy.

Chapter One
Civility

AN UGLY TOAD *decided one day that he could cure all the illnesses that plagued his neighbors in his small community. The toad held himself out as a wise toad trained in the art of healing.*

One day, a fox, impressed by the toad's reputation, sought him out for some advice about curing an illness. But when the fox laid eyes on the toad he noticed that the toad appeared to be crippled. Moreover, he was

15

bloated and fat and had unhealthy-looking blotches all over his skin. The fox decided not to ask for advice from the fat old toad. Instead, he explained to the toad that it did not make much sense to listen to his advice until the toad could show that he could cure himself of his own obvious illnesses.

In recent years, the topic *de jour* for judges' conferences and state bar meetings has been incivility and the demise of dignity in our profession. Typically, this judge or that judge stands in front of a room full of judges and lawyers and states what should be obvious to any lawyer who has engaged in discovery, hearings, or trials in the past decade. The speaker generally talks about our "duty to the court," our "duty to the bar." Occasionally, the speaker will contemplate our "duty to the republic." In most of those conferences, you can occasionally hear a sigh of anguish or frustration that at least gives the appearance of genuine soul searching taking place. Occasionally some senior member of the bar will stand and give the crowd a short reminder of the "good old days" when lawyers respected one another. Perhaps a young lawyer might feel shamed into giving a quick "we can do better" speech that often digresses into little more than a bumper-sticker formula for kind and courteous behavior. Still, at the end of that conference, another Monday morning will come, and our republic, our justice system, will rock on unchanged and unimproved.

On Monday morning following that conference, a lawyer somewhere in America will stretch, bend, or blatantly violate commonsense rules about right and wrong. At judges' and lawyers' conferences, we may

refer to that lawyer's conduct as "incivility." When we are really honest with ourselves, however, we begin to recognize that "incivility" as it is understood these days really is a code word for lying, cheating, sometimes stealing. Because on Monday morning somewhere in America, a large corporation will pay some hungry, aggressive lawyer the right amount of money to change his job description from lawyer to lapdog. On Monday morning, some plaintiffs' lawyer will convince herself that her malingering client is really not a malingerer, that her client really does deserve a day in court, that it is *not* about fees. So we pursue money in preference to justice. We practice law as a trade, rather than as a profession.

Replacing Enlightenment with Enmity

In the 1830s, Alexis de Tocqueville took a hard look at the inner workings of democracy in America. He concluded that lawyers during that time formed a class of people that he described as "enlightened." He said he had found a group of professionals in America that the "people do not mistrust." This is the same group of professionals that people *do* mistrust today. The same group of professionals that Americans trust about as much as politicians, used car salespersons, and pawnbrokers. We have come a long way in less than 200 years.

We would have to be blind not to recognize that incivility in the way we interact among ourselves and the way we interact with the rest of the world is at least partially to blame for the demise of that image de Tocqueville described in the 1830s.

This book chapter does not confuse the notion of civility with a "Miss Manners" type of etiquette designed to instruct genteel members of the bar in how to address the court. Rather, the discussion of civility and incivility as contemplated in this chapter is much more raw and basic. Incivility as contemplated in this chapter is more closely aligned with acts of lying and cheating—with the act of becoming pathetic, boorish, lapdogs for the highest bidders. Miss Manners cannot offer meaningful advice for how to move on from where we are as lawyer professionals today.

The nineteenth-century novelist Herman Melville penned powerful words that we should pay attention to today. He wrote:

We can no longer simply act for ourselves, for our lives are connected by a thousand invisible threads. Our actions run as causes and return to us as results.

Steve Bozeman, a Mississippi lawyer, puts a spin on Melville's "invisible thread metaphor " this way:

We have a handful of attorneys in our community of lawyers of the type that can no doubt be found in almost every local bar association throughout America. They are lawyers who have sold out on the idea that they can zealously honor their duty to their client without bastardizing the truth beyond recognition. They are lawyers who have an inability to say simply "No, I am unwilling to take your money because I do not believe in you or your case." They are the lawyers who use catchy phrases like, "professional duty" or "ethical obligation" to rationalize that their conduct—no matter how uncivil, no matter how dishonest or mean-spirited—somehow falls within their job description. They are lawyers who could never be convinced that the way they regard basic values such as civility, fairness, honesty, and integrity in the way they practice law in even the smallest of cases really does impact the orderly governance of our entire republic. After three years of law school, after 10, 20, even 30 years of practicing law, it never becomes clear to them that they are not the tail wagging the dog—they are the dog.

"Decency Still Matters" — Lee Atwater

In the 1980s, Lee Atwater was the man to see for any politician looking for a political attack dog. Atwater had a reputation for being willing to destroy the good name of decent people in order to win a close contest. He candidly admitted that, for the right price, he would distort facts and warp the truth to whatever degree was necessary to win. At the height of Atwater's career as a political handler, he was quick to point out that civility and decency did not have a place of importance in the political arena. Atwater had convinced himself that the end always justified the means. Blind, aggressive ambition had caused Atwater to lose his way in this world in and out of his role as political advisor. He had lost sight of what really matters. He had developed a philosophy of confrontational engagement that made the Machiavellis and the Nietzsches of this world seem kind and gentle.

In 1990, Atwater suddenly collapsed as he stood at a lectern delivering a speech. Within days, he learned that he was engaged in a battle that he could not win. At the very pinnacle of his career, after being paid millions of dollars as a consultant, after being anointed as the prince of attack-dog politics, he was told that a cancerous tumor growing in his brain would soon end his life.

In the short time between diagnosis and death, Atwater had the opportunity to critically review what mattered and what *should* have mattered to him in his 40-year life. He believed that his conclusions were important enough to be memorialized in moving interviews conducted shortly before his death. In those interviews, Atwater concluded that ends do not always justify their means. The message he delivered in those interviews was like a restatement of principles we could easily find in the Torah, the New Testament, the Koran, or the Upanishads. He restated principles about living that should matter to any attorney wanting to occupy the high ground in the way he or she lives and lawyers.

In the end, Atwater concluded that civility and decency should have had a place of importance in all parts of his life, both in and out of politics. He pointed out that distorting the truth in our professional lives is no less harmful than distorting and bastardizing the truth in our interaction with our spouses, our children, or our friends and neighbors.

The advice left by Lee Atwater can best be paraphrased this way: "We cannot live one way in the way we make a living in this world and another way in the way we interact with our children, friends, and neighbors." Atwater finally understood what is not always obvious even when we are paying attention. He finally understood that there is an interconnection between all the many parts and subparts of our lives. In lawyering terms, that truth might be stated this way: We cannot dishonestly shred documents for a shifty, mendacious client on Monday and offer much meaningful leadership for family the other six days of the week.

From the moment we start our first job as lawyers, many of us become so committed to that long journey to the top of the heap that we quit paying attention to the rest of the world. Our vision becomes myopic and our hearing tunes in to only the loud rumbling and shrill pitches often heard in confrontation. We fail to see and hear the enlightened wisdom of those who have made that journey before us. We fail to pay attention to the Lee Atwaters of this world who are trying to make us hear and see what we already know in our head and feel in our hearts: that the *way* we live our lives in *all* parts and subparts of our lives really does matter.

Causes of Incivility

Donald McCullough tackled the topic of incivility in an interesting book entitled *Say Please, Say Thank You.* Like other scholars and authors who have explored this subject, he tried to determine the root causes of incivility. His distilled thoughts come down to this: Postmodern culture is plagued with incivility because:

1. There are too many of us;
2. We have overworked and stressed ourselves out to the point that we are too tired to be decent human beings;
3. We have become numb to the impact of "shock"; and
4. We have convinced ourselves that kindness and gentleness are character qualities for losers.

Too many of us? Too tired to be decent? Shock-numb? Are those, in part, the causes of incivility among lawyers?

Too Many Lawyers

In the past three decades, more than 50 new law schools have opened their doors. Law schools bring an influx of money to colleges and universities, so the appeal of opening a new school of law or of expanding the existing one is almost irresistible to academic institutions. The result of this is that we now have a crowded profession.

If you ever have the desire to initiate a discussion that will stir up a room full of lawyers, you might begin by declaring that there are too many of us. Suggest that there should be a moratorium on new law schools and that existing law schools should dramatically reduce their new enrollments. You will immediately see the lawyers in that room divide into three general groups. One group will be the lawyers who are administrators, professors, or in some way the beneficiaries of the business of legal education. Another group will be the number-crunching managing partners of mid-size to very large law firms. The third group will be solo practitioners and members of smaller law firms.

Opinions about this topic, much like opinions about most topics, will be driven primarily by self-interest. Members of the law school industry will become indignant. Big-firm managing partners will panic. Solo practitioners and lawyers in small firms will declare that you are a prophet. You will quickly see that building a consensus for the proposition that there are too many of us is much like herding dozens of wild alley cats up a steep hill.

I practice law in an area that is situated between two counties. One county is distinctly different from the other. One is the "old guard" county where the atmosphere is relaxed and business is done with a handshake. The other county is flush with new lawyers because we have two active law schools in the area. There is more panic on the faces of these new lawyers because of their need to get and develop business. They want to survive, but they are getting clients that maybe they really do not want but feel they need to take in order to keep their business alive.

That observation by Betsy Wakefield, a solo practitioner from Vermilion, Ohio, in no way resembles what a law school dean or a big-firm managing partner would have to say about the topic.

The law school dean would argue that almost 40,000 new lawyers graduating every year are still not enough to service America's needs. That same dean certainly would argue that new graduates are bringing more diversity to the stodgy old white men's club that the legal profession has for so long been. Also, one statistic that you are sure to hear from the folks in the law school business is that roughly 70 percent of the lawyers in America devote their lives to serving only 20 percent of the population needing legal assistance.

Small accredited, unaccredited, partially accredited law schools, night law schools, even correspondence law school programs, all employ professors and deans who will be slow to admit that they are flooding the market with new lawyers who are barely making a living in communities all over this country. The people who are now in the business of law school education will be slow to admit that they have helped create the monstrous gap in quality of compensation that exists between graduates of established, more prestigious law schools and graduates of newer, little-known law schools that have become part of the law education business. The big firms will continue hiring Ivy League graduates for six-figure starting salaries, and graduates from the vast majority of the "other" law schools will test their resolve to make a living with their license. Every one of these small, lesser-known schools will have a collection of tales of the graduate who made good, the graduate who is now listed in *The Best Lawyers in America* or is a member of the International Academy of Trial Lawyers or the like.

The placement departments in most of those schools will spout statistics about how all their graduates are gainfully employed in some form or fashion. They will gloat about the starting salary of the graduates who finished in the top 20 percent of their class. But still, when you talk to most of the remaining 80 percent of the class, the picture is not so rosy.

Too many of the new entrepreneurial law schools that see good profit margins in the "business" of law school education create false hopes for the less fortunate 90 percent of their graduates.

Reality for too many of those graduates falls far short of the expectations they began developing the day they received their first admission booklet in the mail telling them about the endless possibilities available to the graduate of *(fill in the blank)* School of Law.

Dick Warfield has some first-hand observations about the impact of too many lawyers:

When I first hung my shingle more than 40 years ago, there were about 50 lawyers practicing in the four-county area where I live. We not only knew each other's names; we knew spouses' names and children's names. There are too many of us these days. All of us scrambling for the same opportunity, the same dollar. The looks we give each other are almost predatory in some settings—lean and hungry. There is no kinship, no connection with each other as lawyers, much less as friends and neighbors.

We used to understand that there are many costs to "winning at all costs." One cost used to be that the lawyer who wanted only to win regardless of the cost to the system, the cost to the process, usually ended up burning bridges with his friends, his colleagues, his peers. Burning bridges like that used to mean something, but now there are so many of us that we have minimized the importance of civility. Civility becomes secondary to competition within our escalating numbers. We used to understand that the way we lived among ourselves as lawyers had tremendous impact on our entire society.

Has Warfield put his finger on the root cause of the problem? Or at least a portion of it? Is it that our profession has become so crowded that we must fight and scrap among ourselves for mere survival? Or for what we think is our due? Perhaps out-of-control growth is at least one of the causes of our dilemma.

Not only do the people in the "business" of law schools want more law graduates, America's biggest law firms want them too. More and bigger has always translated to dollar signs for America's largest firms.

In the movie *Jerry McGuire,* Tom Cruise plays the role of an attorney who makes his living as a sports agent. His character, McGuire, undertakes the creation of a mission statement that he believes should change the way sports agents do business. Cruise's fictional character has visions of a kinder, gentler way of conducting business. The pivotal part of that mission statement created by McGuire is that agents need to represent fewer clients and resign themselves to making less money. McGuire concludes that only then can the sports agent profession arrive at a place where agents are adequately serving the needs of their clients.

McGuire created a mission statement that is inconsistent with the goals of America's mega-firms. The year that movie was filmed the average billable hours for the typical attorney in a large law firm reached between 2,000 and 2,200 hours per year. In other words, the lawyers who, with a straight face, were submitting the 2,200-hour time cards were saying that they had worked six days a week, eleven hours per day, all year long. In fact, in many larger city firms, it is common to have lawyers who report 3,000 or more hours per year. The managing partners of America's big firms have figured out how to make young lawyers graduating from law school into a cheap, profitable commodity. They are turning the labor of easily expendable young associates into bigger profit margins. When more law schools turn out more law school graduates, then big law firms have a bigger work force creating more and bigger billable hours.

A friend of mine sent me an interesting cartoon several years ago. It was the picture of a plump young associate caged up in the same type of cattle stall that beef producers use to fatten up young calves for the production of veal. The message of the cartoon was obvious. The message was that the intellect and labor of young, talented law school graduates is being treated like a cheapened commodity by the new mega-sized law firms that must overbill in order to keep their doors open.

In 1999, the *ABA Journal* explored the "billing boom" in a cover story entitled "Cash-and-Carry Associates." The author, Debra Baker, told the story of how the best and the brightest Generation Xers are choosing not to stay long in firms that are turning their intellect and their time into a commodity. The attrition rate for new associates in big firms is consistently in the range of one out of two within the first four years of practice. The widget assembly line concept of lawyering in big firms seems like a good idea for the highly compensated partner in charge of aggressive and creative billing for the firm, but it apparently does not seem to many new associates like a workable way to lawyer. The good news is that there are real live Jerry McGuires out there within the ranks of new lawyers. Quality of living and lawyering does matter. They do have the class and character to buy into a mission statement that includes "fewer clients, less money."

Too Tired to Be Civil

When Donald McCullough theorizes that our culture as a whole has become too stressed, too tired, too overwhelmed to be civil, it sounds an awful lot like what might be happening within our smaller culture of lawyers. In the last several years, there has been a dramatic increase in the numbers of new organizations that devote their energies to helping lawyers cope with the struggle of lawyering. Lawyer assistance programs that identify themselves with names such as Lawyers Concerned for Lawyers and Lawyers Helping Lawyers are compiling statistics that would suggest to even the casual observer that we are not in the frame of mind that lends itself to civility within our group. These groups are telling us that when we compare lawyers to the rest of America's population, our rate of alcohol abuse and serious depression and anxiety is substantially higher than that of the rest of the population.

An article by the director of the New Jersey Lawyers' Assistance Program recently appeared in *The New Jersey Lawyer*. The publishers set out to catch readers' attention with the following copy printed in bold type on the first page of the article:

One out of every four lawyers suffers from elevated feelings of psychological distress. The primary complaints are, in order, interpersonal feelings of inadequacy and inferiority, anxiety, social alienation/ isolation and depression.

Out of 105 occupations, lawyers ranked first in depression.

**A total of 45 percent of lawyers feel they
do not have enough family time and 54
percent say they do not have enough time
for themselves.**

Mark Proctor, a workers' compensation lawyer in
Florida, believes that a host of negative things such
as those listed above happen when you have too
many lawyers working far too hard for the same piece
of cheese:

> I recall some of the basic principles I learned
> in my early college sociology and psychology
> classes. Those principles were typically illustrated
> by overcrowding a cage with too many gerbils or
> rats and studying the changes that took place
> among whatever furry little creatures occupied
> that cage. The general rule of thumb was that as
> crowding, cramming, and increased competition
> for furry little animal food increased, so did the
> levels of stress, hostility, intolerance, and general

enmity within that uncomfortable caged community. My memory was that the fast-paced competition for a greater share of existing food and space and control of that cage always brought out the worst in its occupants. At the end of the day in that cage, its occupants were too tired to exhibit much attention or concern for each other. More often than not, the community of lawyers practicing in my back yard display most of the same characteristics that took place with those anxious furry creatures in crowded cages.

I truly believe that, for the most part, the type of malaise described above is self-inflicted. We are not able to accept the type of professional mission statement that leads us to being content, and in turn we run ourselves as ragged as rats in a small cage. We condition ourselves to habitually reach for more than we really need to live peacefully, comfortably, and securely. We place ourselves squarely in a world that tires us out, stresses us out, and depletes our energy to the point that we have nothing left to devote to acts of civility. Civility becomes just as unimportant to us as it is to a cage full of rats competing for the same piece of cheese.

Dumbing Down the Way We Look

Martin Levin has practiced law 15 years. In those years, he says he has seen an entire "entertainment" industry develop around talking-head lawyers clamoring for the opportunity to shock their way into prime time. Levin writes:

> I was channel surfing one night and realized that on 5 of the 60 television stations available to me in my area there were lawyers screaming at each other about who was right and who was wrong about everything from politics to search and seizure. There was a moderately attractive blond lawyer on one station who went to great lengths to impress upon the viewers that she had nothing but

disdain for the office of the presidency. She snarled and alternated between shaking her finger at the camera and pounding her hand on the table in front of her. She looked childish and foolish. It was a scene that would have been amusing and laughable had I been watching a post–wrestling match commentary. But I was watching a talking-head lawyer commentary. On another station, I saw a lawyer almost jumping out of his three-piece suit verbally attacking a black judge about that judge's position on racism in America. The judge, wanting to gain an upper hand, chose to scream back.

As I watched the histrionics, the demagoguery, the self-promotion, the lack of intellect, the absolute disrespect for one another that was taking place on that television screen, it occurred to me that these legal pundits weren't attempting to educate me, inspire me, or help me in any way as a viewer. No, their goal was to shock me in hopes that I would tune them in tomorrow night.

Lawyers have become the new "shock jocks" of the television airways. They will say and do damn near anything to get fifteen minutes of air time on a talking heads program. Television and radio producers have found large numbers of trial lawyers, legal scholars, and legal pundits who are willing to scream into cameras, to humiliate, debase, and generally cheapen their opponents, themselves, and their entire profession in exchange for fifteen minutes of fleeting face time. Shock is what the media producers count on for ratings, and they are able to find far too many within our ranks who are willing to deliver those shock scripts like trained circus monkeys.

We really do not need to turn on our television sets, however, to watch the Howard Stern type of escalating shock. We can go sit through depositions and watch one side attempt to outshock the other by ranting and raving at each other and at deponents, only because some maladjusted or mean-spirited client expects that from his lawyer. For a few dollars, that client has found a lawyer willing to deliver.

Or we can sit in courtrooms almost anywhere in America and listen to presiding judges allowing their sense of power and importance to overcome their judicial demeanor. We can watch judges scream at our clients and scream at us simply because their fragile ego has been somehow offended. We can observe the most pivotally important person in the courtroom taking on the demeanor of Judge Judy and abandoning any attempt to lead with wisdom, experience, and character.

In those same courtrooms, we can also occasionally watch lawyers provide a kind of sideshow service for their clients in front of juries.

Jackie Rion practices law in South Carolina. His thoughts might help us transform absurdity into insight:

> I heard about a lawyer in Georgia who ate a cockroach in front of a jury to make the point that the roach that the plaintiff had swallowed as she drank out of the defendant's bottle had been thoroughly sterilized and created no physical harm to the plaintiff. Apparently, one of the jurors became ill and had to be excused,

and at some point before the hungry lawyer popped another sterile roach into his mouth, the judge intervened and cautioned that one roach was enough. In the end, the insurance defense lawyer walked away with a defense verdict.

The judge regained control of his courtroom, and the juror recovered and no doubt has retold her story about the cockroach-eating lawyer hundreds of times. I wondered how much that lawyer had been paid by his "master" to eat a cockroach. I wondered if in another life that person who happened to have a law degree might just as easily have been a tattooed man in a freak show or an ape man in a traveling circus if the promoter offered to pay the right amount of money. I wondered what he must have been thinking to have done that to my profession.

Kind and Gentle Lawyers Are Losers?

The book *Skadden: Power, Money, and the Rise of a Legal Empire* was written about a law firm whose name from time to time appears in books, journals, and articles discussing the lack of civility in the legal profession. The author, Lincoln Caplan, spent almost five years researching the inner workings of the firm and in fact had been granted access even to closed-door meetings that took place within the organization that at one time was one of America's wealthiest law firms.

History has shown us that mega-firms like Skadden will come and go, but as they come and go, how are they shaping our lawyering culture in regard to civility?

"I'm at Skadden Arps now. We pride ourselves on being assholes. It's part of the firm culture." This quotation from Caplan's book was attributed to a Skadden lawyer. The statement was made as she sat on an A.B.A. panel assembled to discuss litigation techniques.

Psychologists will tell us that when people openly discuss their most unattractive, unsavory, malevolent, or sordid personal qualities, they typically only show us the tip of the iceberg. If that is true, then we should at least devote some analysis to this little anecdotal event.

One question that might come to your mind as you think about this event is this: Even though in her mind she worked around a "culture" of lawyers who she believed were proud to be "assholes," was she personally proud to characterize herself as an "asshole," or was she making such a statement to appear more severe and hardened—maybe even less vulnerable than the other lawyer participants at that conference? If she could convincingly adopt a toxic-looking persona, did she better equip herself to survive within her firm's culture and the lawyer culture at large? Maybe she actually believed she would look less like a loser.

The Evolution of the Lapdog

Wesley J. Smith and Ralph Nader, in their book *No Contest,* use the term "legal Darwinism" to describe the escalating problems of the almost sickly incivility that pervades the practice of law today. Most writers who are critically observing our profession's "evolution" are concluding that the type of culture that the Skadden lawyer was saying was alive and well at her firm is not aberrational but may in fact be a permanent adaptation for our entire lawyer species. The reasons for this type of evolution are not complicated or mysterious. They may even be summarized as simply as this:

- Huge numbers of lawyers began raising their financial expectations higher and higher (they became greedy).

- Huge numbers of lawyers realized that attracting more clients, bigger clients, helped them satisfy those financial expectations (satisfy their greed).

- Huge numbers of lawyers began to realize that those clients were not interested in hiring wise, intellectual, well-rounded counselors. What they really wanted was a mongrel-like lapdog.

- The characteristics of the lapdog then began taking form. The qualities most clients were looking for in a lapdog were a bad disposition, threatening-looking teeth, healthy claws, savage cunning, and an abundance of venal tendencies.

- As those lapdog features began to evolve, left behind were all traces of qualities that made the "evolved" legal lapdog appear vulnerable or naive. Qualities such as wisdom, geniality, generosity, refined intellect, civility, trustworthiness, idealism, and honesty atrophied as the course of natural selection progressed.

Looking Beyond Blame

It is popular nowadays to place most of the blame for an uncivil justice system at the feet of law schools. First, the argument is that even America's best law schools have attracted professors who develop a need-to-know curriculum to help students pass state bar exams. That need-to-know type of teaching is not in any way geared to forming or reforming students' values, attitudes, or motivations in regard to such things as civility, altruism, fair dealing, ambition, social responsibility, materialism, philosophy of competition, or balanced living. The attitude of most professors is that it is a bar exam the law student must prepare for, not a Myers-Briggs–type personality and character test. Critics who begin their blame game at the front door of our law schools suggest that the folks in charge of teaching lawyers to think like lawyers are most of the time woefully out of touch with just how serious the crisis of lawyer incivility has become in "the world."

The second and more cynical part of the failing law school argument is that law schools are attracting law students who couldn't care less about rehabilitating our profession or our civil justice system. The argument is that the typical law student for the past several decades has been motivated more by money than any abiding moral or philosophical motivation to improve our justice system or our profession. In other words, the critic argues that most law school graduates leave law school looking for the highest-paying jobs regardless of what that high-paying employer asks them to do for that premium money.

The unfortunate aspect of the failing law school/failing law student argument is that it allows the 800,000 of us already practicing law to willingly, in fact gratefully, abdicate our responsibility to show leadership in rebuilding an honorable profession.

Passing the buck has rarely solved serious problems in any organization, and it will not prevent the continuing demise of civility in our profession.

The overwhelming majority of law school graduates are not inclined to become morally lame, fierce-looking lapdogs when they graduate from law school. If that is what some of them become, it is because older, experienced lawyers in key positions of leadership in firms all over America have dropped the ball in their capacity as leaders.

David McCormick, a true lawyer's lawyer from Mississippi, has his view about who might share some part of the responsibility;

The legal profession is at a place where too many of the people who should be showing leadership are driven by a "what's in it for me" attitude. As a result, the public has figured out that lawyers make up a profession that is on the verge of becoming dysfunctional because of insane incivility.

I have been a plaintiffs' lawyer most of my career, and I would like to say that it is only the big corporate defense firms that are failing to toe the leadership line. I would prefer to argue that they alone are targeting, recruiting, and hiring the most mean-spirited, Machiavellian, mercenary law school graduates. It makes me more comfortable to believe that only the 200-lawyer corporate defense firms dedicated to setting new billing records are the ones tutoring young lawyers in the ways of incivility for profit. But that is not true. Senior partners within the typical plaintiffs' firm these days are usually proud of the number of young trial lawyer attack dogs they have trained and penned up around their shop. Qualities such as altruism, kindliness, idealism, and compassion are not qualities that make lawyers an attractive hire at most plaintiffs' firms these days. Let's face it: all sides of our profession have made incivility profitable.

Young lawyers right out of law school are adapting to ways that we have developed for them. Most of the time when their conduct as a lawyer minimizes decency, it is because they believe that some older, more experienced lawyer might actually approve of what they are doing.

The legal profession can solve its civility crisis only when the people at the top of America's law firms solve their own very ugly, very personal crisis, which evolves from their greed.

Aesop used an insightful fable to explain to the leaders of his day that moving from the point of recognizing a threat to the point of taking the necessary action to vanquish that threat was an almost impossible move for poorly adjusted leaders. It often requires too much courage.

There was once a fierce-looking cat that regularly threatened a group of mice. The cat had long claws and sharp teeth, but even more dangerous was the cat's ability to move so stealthily and silently that the mice were unable to hear or see it coming. It threatened the entire mouse community.

One day the mice leaders met to devise a solution to the cat problem. No good plans were suggested until one of the mice pointed out that if they could simply hang a bell around the cat's neck, then they would be able to hear the cat coming in time to hide.

All the other mice thought that the idea was the perfect first step for solving their cat problem. The small group of mice rejoiced and again and again proclaimed how helpful the bell warning would be. After long hours of talk, however, one mouse brought an end to the festive mood by asking a tough question. The mouse asked, "Who will bell the cat?"

Too often, lawyer and judge association meetings take on the qualities of the "Mice in Council" described in Aesop's fable. Experienced and often venerated leaders of our bar and our judiciary prophesy the demise of our profession. They make plausible arguments about how we can and must regain the high ground in public opinion. They lecture about how greed and avarice are at the root of incivility. They talk about the possibility that there may be too many of us. They declare that older lawyers need to provide better mentoring of younger lawyers. They argue that we are no longer a service profession, and then they end their speech leaving you to wonder, "Who is going to show enough character and courage to get that bell around the cat's neck?"

Chapter Two
Cultural Disconnect

W HEN THE TOWN MOUSE *visited his country cousin, the simple lunch he was served consisted of wheat stalks, roots, acorns, and plain water. The town mouse ate a bite or two, just to be polite, but he had expected more from a meal. After the modest meal, the town mouse bragged about his life in the big city while the country mouse listened. Then they fell asleep in the country mouse's comfortable nest, which was nestled beneath a hedgerow.*

As they slept, the country mouse dreamed of living in the luxury described by his cousin. So when the morning came and the town mouse invited the country mouse to come to the city, he gladly accepted.

When they reached the great house the town mouse called home, they found the remains of a grand banquet awaiting them. The country mouse had a hard time deciding where to begin. He was surrounded by cheeses, pastries, breads, and fine wine.

Just as he was heading for a hunk of cheese, he heard a very big cat clawing at the door. Both mice scurried to a safe hiding place and waited in terrified silence as the danger passed.

After a long wait, they decided it was safe to venture out again, but at that moment, the door burst open. It was the servants coming to clear the table, and with them was a huge, ferocious-looking dog.

The country mouse ran from the house to return to his comfortable hedgerow. As he left, he told the town mouse, "I am not willing to trade the peace and calm I have in my life for all the luxuries you have to offer."

Most of us hear very big cats clawing at our door throughout most of the years we practice law. Unlike the country mouse, we do not have the luxury of escaping to a safe and comfortable hedgerow every time we are confronted by some huge, ferocious-looking dog threatening us and our clients. Most of us clearly understand the advantages of finding for ourselves as much peace and calm as we possibly can in a tumultuous world. But the truth is that some of us are better than others at finding peace and calm in the midst of the chaos that attaches itself to day to day lawyering.

Modern authors of self-help books routinely borrow and modify the commonsense approaches to simplifying life that Henry David Thoreau wrote about more than 150 years ago. Walk into most book stores and you will find books with titles such as *Living the Simple Life, Simplify Your Life, and Urban Serenity: 14 Ways to Simplify your Life.* As you walk past those books, walk a little farther to the part of the bookstore where the classics are on display.

Pick up almost anything ever written by Thoreau, and you will see some fairly consistent themes about simplifying our lives through what can best be described as a type of cultural disconnect. In one of his lectures late in his life, Thoreau said:

I think that I cannot preserve my health and spirits, unless I spend four hours a day at least—and it is commonly more than that—sauntering through the woods and over the hills and fields, absolutely free from all worldly engagements. ...When sometimes I am reminded that the mechanics and shopkeepers stay in their shops not only all the forenoon, but all the afternoon too, sitting with crossed legs, so many of them—as if the legs were made to sit upon and not to stand or walk upon—I think that they deserve some credit for not having all committed suicide long ago.... I confess that I am astonished at the power of endurance, to say nothing of the moral insensibility, of my neighbors who confine themselves to shops and offices the whole day for weeks and months, aye, and years almost together. I know not what manner of stuff they are of, sitting there now at three o'clock in the afternoon, as if it were three o'clock in the morning.

Hardly any of us have the time or opportunity to take four hours each day for a saunter into the wilderness to escape the stresses, turmoil, and sometimes downright chaos that confronts us on most days lawyering. However, that does not mean that the principles that Thoreau was preaching throughout his many years of writing and lecturing have no relevance to our lawyering lives.

When we synthesize the most important ideas of what Thoreau typically preached about, they come down to some pretty basic guidelines that cover what should be our rules for engagement in our day-to-day living.

Those basic rules for engagement can be listed as follows:

1. Live deliberately.
2. Disconnect from the culture and the daily grind as often as possible.
3. Grow spiritually.

Live Deliberately

There is a popular misconception that Thoreau was a recluse, that he was so repulsed by his contemporary culture that he was willing to live the life of a hermit in the forest, next to a pond. If Thoreau were alive and living alone somewhere deep in a forest in a small log cabin in the year 2000, he would no doubt be regarded as an eccentric dropout. We might refer to him as a shiftless, indolent slacker, maybe even a fragile, oversensitive neurotic who simply could not cope.

It is true that Thoreau did not love the culture he was a part of, but it is wrong to imagine that that culture scared him into the woods. Thoreau said this about his trip to the woods:

> I went to the woods because I wished to
> live deliberately, to front only the essential
> facts of life, and see if I could not learn what it
> had to teach, and not, when I came to die,
> discover that I had not lived.

Plenty has been written about what Thoreau meant when he said that he wanted to live "deliberately." Janet

Luhrs, author of the book *The Simple Living Guide,* believes that Thoreau was telling us that he wanted to make a well-defined, conscious decision, a deliberate decision about the way he chose to live. Luhrs is a lawyer who no longer has an active practice. Instead, she publishes the journal *Simple Living: The Journal of Voluntary Simplicity.* She is a regular guest on National Public Radio, where she is often heard giving wise yet practical advice about how we can improve our lives. This quotation helps explain her concept of "deliberate" living:

> I've chosen to have kids' science projects, newspapers, and my sister's slippers cluttering the living room rather than living an austere existence. Someone else might like austerity because it brings a sense of peace and order. Either way, we've chosen these things consciously—they don't just "happen."
> Simple living is about making deliberate, thoughtful choices. The difference is that you are fully aware of why you are living your

particular life, and that life is one you have chosen thoughtfully.

The country mouse made a deliberate decision when he told his cousin the town mouse that he was not willing to trade his peace and calm under his hedgerow for all the luxuries and fine food that the big city had to offer. The difference between the country mouse and probably a majority of our brother and sister lawyers is that we are too quick to pursue luxuries without making a conscious, deliberate evaluation of the resulting costs to ourselves and our families.

Patrick Schiltz is an ethics professor at Notre Dame Law School. He is different from the vast majority of ethics professors in that he actually struggled with the rigors of practicing law with a large law firm for many years. In 1999, he wrote an article for the *Vanderbilt Law Review* that covered this subject matter: "Being a Happy, Healthy, and Ethical Member of an Unhappy, Unhealthy, and Unethical Profession."

The article is footnoted to a point verging on what might be regarded as burdensome reading, but the substance of the advice Schiltz has to give is a restatement of Thoreau's advice on deliberate living.

Schiltz's first thesis, supported by a collection of impressive statistics, is this: Among lawyers, there is an inordinately high level of anxiety, depression, alcohol and drug abuse, and divorce. He notes and footnotes—and footnotes—studies and statistics that are indicia of a profession that is overwhelmed by unhappiness, job dissatisfaction, disillusionment, fatigue, burnout, and an overall shabby quality of life.

Once you work your way through more than 380 footnotes, Schiltz finally discards his professional statistical analysis and speaks in the voice of a true-to-life veteran trial lawyer who has been there. Schiltz provides fabulous mentor-like advice in the voice of an older trial lawyer who sincerely cares about the well-being of the 40,000 new young lawyers who will enter this profession this year.

Schiltz provides the following sane advice for any lawyer, young or old, who is still wise enough to learn:

Do not permit yourself to be purchased at auction like a prize hog at the county fair. Do not choose one law firm over another because of a $3,000 difference in starting salaries. Instead, make it clear to prospective employers that salary is only one of many factors that you will consider in choosing a law firm. And then, back up your words with your actions. If the past twenty years had seen one law school graduate intent on living a balanced life for every law school graduate intent on chasing the highest salary, big firms would be very different places today.

When we permit ourselves to be "purchased like a prize hog at the county fair," Schiltz suggests, we lose control over our lives both inside and outside our law office. It doesn't just happen that every day in America a lawyer wakes up and finds that she is upside-down in her professional life as well as her personal life and her spiritual life. It doesn't just mystically happen that five years into her practice a lawyer finds herself churning billable hours to levels that preclude her from ever enjoying the luxuries that she has been able to purchase. It is not an accident that she is overworked, overstressed, overly fearful, and often spiritually over the hill by the time she is ten years into the practice of law.

A long series of deliberate, conscious, decisions put her there…it didn't just happen.

Lawyers are too often unable to understand what the country mouse immediately recognized about the life of the town mouse—that the town mouse was so attached to the idea of surrounding himself with luxuries that he was unable to acknowledge the disorder and chaos, the lack of calm and peacefulness that came with those luxuries.

In order to do what the country mouse did, leaving all that cheese, cake, and wine on the table and fleeing for his comfortable home, he had to have some core values—some personal priorities that he was unable to easily abandon. He had to have developed a mission statement that allowed him to make deliberate decisions about what he was willing to do and what he was unwilling to do. He had to have predetermined what type of day-to-day living he found acceptably comfortable. When his day-to-day living got too far away from that comfort zone, he had to be committed to making deliberate, decisive adjustments.

Archie Lamb practices law in Birmingham. He is of the opinion that we gradually become so dependent on all the trappings of our lawyer culture that we barely notice any of the harmful side affects that that culture brings to our lives.

I remember a story that was told to me when I was a teenager. It was a time when I had been getting into more than my share of trouble. I was told about the frog that had made his way into the kitchen of a house and jumped into a big pot of water that was sitting on the stove. When the frog jumped in, the water was a comfortable room temperature, and the frog did not notice that there was actually a small flame burning underneath the big pot of water. The water heated up gradually but steadily to the point of boiling before the frog at last realized that he must escape from the pot if he wanted to save himself. The happy ending was that the frog made it out of the boiling water with only minor injuries.

I have seen far too many of my friends who graduated from law school with me put themselves in the same predicament as that frog. The scenario goes like this:

Big firm offers big money. The big firm exchanges that money for the lawyer's commitment to bill "only" 2,000 hours or more per year.

The lawyer gets comfortable and pays on some student loans, commits to payments on a new car or a new house; financial freedom at least becomes a possibility after so many years of living like a student.

The big firm then raises billable hour expectations to 2,500...then 3,000. Within the first two years, the big firm has increased demands on the lawyer by small, almost imperceptible degrees.

The lawyer sacrifices physical, mental, and spiritual health, personal relationships, quality of life so he can be on the road traveling 200 days a year, work 80 hours a week, and hold onto a belief that things will change as soon as he is made partner.

I am certain that the frog had a better chance of escaping the pot of boiling water than the average lawyer who has made it to that point in his career.

Disconnect from the Culture

Elaine St. James is the author of a book entitled *Simplify Your Life.* In one section of that book, she puts a modernized spin on Thoreau's advice to occasionally disconnect from civilization as best you can. Thoreau came back from two years of virtual seclusion in the woods with the advice that we should "live in each season" as those seasons come and go. He told us that he learned that it was important to "breathe the air, drink the drink, and taste the fruit and rcsign [ourselves] to the influences of each."

St. James is of the opinion that we don't need to live in some secluded woods every day of our life to improve the way we live day to day. However, a synthesis of her modern spin on an old theory is that we need to try the equivalent of an extended culture fast from time to time. If we are reading three news magazines a week, then stop: we don't need to be that immersed in world news. If we are watching 10 hours of television every week, then stop. St. James explains that disconnecting yourself from the more than $125 billion that advertisers spend each year on television commercials helps you to stop focusing on what our modern culture tells you to think, buy, believe, need, ignore, expect, and celebrate. By disconnecting from the television—news shows and all—you allow yourself to disconnect from a great deal of the most superficial qualities of our modern culture.

In preparing to write this book, I sent a questionnaire to a large sampling of lawyers (see Appendix). One of the questions asked in that survey focuses on what effects images that are sold by the media such as magazines, television, or movies actually have on the lifestyles of the lawyer respondents. Twenty-four percent said they have never considered any possible impact on their lives. Sixty percent said they consider trendy people to be weak and impressionable. Fifty-nine percent state that they always recognize that those images are illusory. However, 46 percent still said that those images push them to be more materialistic than they would prefer.

St. James and most others writing about the virtues of simplified living tell us to regularly take extended fasts from our cultural addictions. These writers ask us to reconsider whether or not we really need to strap onto our belts a three-ounce telephone that provides for Call Waiting, Call Forwarding, real-time stock quotes, Caller ID, three-way conference calls, top stories of the day, etc. In fact, they go so far as to tell us to do the unthinkable: "Don't answer the phone just because it is ringing."

Here is the practical problem for what Thoreau and modern "simple living" theorists have to say about cultural disconnect: Most of us are physically and mentally unable to disconnect for one day, much less periods extending beyond 30 days.

Lawyers for the most part are a fairly dedicated group of "control freaks" who are terrified by the idea of disconnecting from any part of civilization for any length of time, no matter how short. We too often really believe that our delicately balanced world requires every moment of the kind of genius, expertise, creativity, magnetism, vigor, and dynamics that only we are equipped to deliver. Chaos will surely result if we fail to answer a phone call, much less intentionally engage in anything that sounds like a culture fast for more than 30 days.

In 1995, a study by three researchers named Beck, Sales, and Benjamin appeared in the *Journal of Law and Health.* That study did not treat the desire of lawyers to overcontrol their world and everybody else's world as simply a cute little affectation. Instead, that study showed that our desire to control may be more problematic for some of us. According to those researchers, 21 percent of the male lawyers followed in that study could be classified as suffering from obsessive-compulsive disorder. The level of obsessive-compulsiveness in the general population, on the other hand, is only 1.24 percent. That, of course, does not mean that all of that obsessing centers only on our need to control, but we all know our share of fellow lawyers who definitely would fit that bill.

It would no doubt be torturous to tell the average obsessing lawyer that he must sit down and read about and maybe even believe some of the simple wisdom Thoreau offers about the advantages of cultural disconnect. Most compulsive, controlling lawyers can't get their minds around the idea that such wisdom might improve their lives.

If you first are able to conclude that clearing the cultural clutter from your day-to-day life might leave more time and more room for a little more peace and calm, then you should take the next step. Read at least one book written by the experts on how to simplify your life.

The difficulty with taking these "simple living" books seriously is that many of them are packed with what could easily be regarded as silly, warm and fuzzy, Oprah-like advice. For example, a collection of chapter topics from a few of those books includes: *(a)* Stop Sending Christmas Cards, *(b)* Don't Answer the Doorbell, *(c)* Don't Open your Mail for Two Days, and *(d)* Replace Your Lawn with Ground Cover.

Your first reaction may be to snicker, squirm in your chair, and dismiss the entire idea of simpler living as irrelevant foolishness. But get over it and force yourself to read on. Force yourself to recognize that, mixed with advice that could be considered Pollyannaish are solid commonsense ideas about overcoming cultural clutter of the same type that Thoreau discovered during his years living next to Walden Pond.

It is unlikely that many of us will ever have the opportunity to test Thoreau's wisdom about cultural disconnect in the manner that he recommends. A four-hour walk into the woods each day stretches the bounds of reality for most of us, and moving into the woods to live in a quaint log cabin by a pond might result in our being institutionalized by our family and close friends. But we can and must recognize and deal with those habits that keep us so squarely, so obsessively, so compulsively "in control."

Allow someone else to be *"in control"* more often; *unclutter* your day-to-day life by shedding some of the culture you have become addicted to: newspapers, magazines, television, movies, radio, telephones, stock quotes, advertisements, and politics. Commit yourself to *downsizing,* downscaling, living on less, owning fewer things, making fewer financial commitments, living below your means. Be as obsessed with planning your time for solitude as you are in planning your work schedule. This is a synthesis of the advice from simpler-living experts who have devoted a huge amount of time and creativity to trying to lead a modern culture at least to the edge of Thoreau's uncluttered woods.

Grow Spiritually

Thoreau believed that the culture of his day did not allow much time for the average citizen to grow spiritually. He recognized that the clamor, the racket, and the clutter that confronted the typical American city dweller in 1839 did not allow for even brief solitude. Thoreau believed that there was a relationship between periods of solitude and spiritual reflection. He told us this about his time at Walden:

> I had three chairs in my house; one for solitude, two for friendship, three for society.

When we practice law with a belief that spiritual growth does not improve our lives, we tend to minimize the importance of the type of solitude that Thoreau believed was so important.

Twentieth-century sociologists during the 1990s began paying attention to a trend among baby boomers. They identified a revitalized focus on spirituality and its relationship to such things as health, family, business, leadership, and happiness. The sociologists tell us that the trend may be driven by the same type of self-centered compulsion that has driven boomers for decades. This compulsion, according to people who have studied yuppy trends for more than 40 years, results from our suddenly becoming extremely conscious of our mortality. Put another way, we are scared as hell that we are closer to the end of a 73-year life than we are to the beginning, and we want to find more to life than our culture has to offer.

In the year 2000, some of America's biggest blue chip corporations are promoting spirituality within their organizations. Boeing is opening its conference rooms up to employees wanting to study the Torah, the Bible, and the Koran during and after work hours. Intel not only permits but promotes Islamic study groups. Bible studies are a regularly occurring event on Northrup Grumman property. You can even participate in Torah classes at Microsoft.

Pop culture magazines such as *Spirituality and Health* tell us that their mission is not to try to win converts to any particular belief system. Rather, they are publications intent on showing us ways to exercise our spirituality as often and as completely as we exercise our minds and bodies.

Critics of this new brand of boomer spirituality, however, argue that boomers are clamoring for the same type of quick-fix, instant-gratification formula that they might expect from the directions on a Rice-a-Roni box. It is spirituality without much solitude, it is rushed religion without reflection that characterizes this hurried, revitalized interest in saving our 40- to 50-year-old souls.

Norman Wright, in his book *Simplify Your Life*, has a chapter entitled "Letting Our Souls Catch Up to Our Bodies." Wright borrowed his idea for the chapter from a passage that appeared in *Springs in the Valley,* a book of daily devotional readings by Mrs. Charles E. Cowman:

In the deep jungles of Africa a traveler was making a long trek. Coolies had been engaged from a tribe to carry the loads. The first day they marched rapidly and went far. The traveler had high hopes of a speedy journey. But the second morning these jungle tribesmen refused to move. For some strange reason they just sat and rested. On inquiry as to the reason for this strange behavior, the traveler was informed that they had gone too fast the first day and that they were now waiting for their souls to catch up with their bodies.

Workdays have gradually become longer and longer for lawyers over the past few decades. A common complaint among most of us is that the time and energy sacrifices we make put many of us in the position of seldom being able to allow our souls to catch up with our bodies. We don't have the good sense to simply sit down like those African porters and admit that we have "gone too fast" or to admit that the rigors of what is going on with our daily lawyering routine have separated us from what is going on with our souls.

It is reasonable to have a belief that the attorney who has made a commitment to sacrifice his life in increments of 80 to 90 hours per week does not have much time to attend to anything resembling spirituality.

Joseph Allegretti practiced labor law in Philadelphia before he became an ethics professor at Creighton University Law School. He is an interesting combination of experienced practitioner, law professor, and theologian. He has written books, essays, and law review articles about how lawyers can avoid allowing their spiritual side to become too separated from the other important parts of their body.

Allegretti defines the problem this way:

> An authentic spirituality resists the temptation
> to become privatized and insular. If the pressures

of legal practice make it difficult for us to serve our clients well, or rob us of time for ourselves and our loved ones, then a reform of law firms and legal institutions is in order. If too many lawyers are living too hectic lives, the solution is not for individuals to slow down and catch their breath (although that would certainly help), but to transform law practice into something more humane. As one writer puts it: "[S]pirituality is about seeking and responding to God's presence. Good policies and humane institutions make it easier to see God. Therefore, far from being a distraction, the reform of institutions is a key ingredient to a spirituality of work."

The idea of transforming the legal profession into something that encourages lawyers to pay more attention to their spiritual side is practical, noble, and very doable. However, it has a few impediments. Greed is one of those impediments. Selfishly obsessed managing partners in mid-sized to large law firms have become taskmasters rather than mentors as they push billable hours higher and higher to further prop up the fiscal standard of living for themselves and the rest of the firm's partners. In their effort to pile up riches for themselves and their firm, these managing taskmasters create a void in their own lives and the lives of the younger lawyers who are making most of the serious personal sacrifices. The cycle then perpetuates itself within most large firms.

There is a reality that is well understood within management circles in corporate America. It is a reality that has the potential to either positively or negatively influence the character of an entire corporation regardless of size. The reality is this: The leadership of an organization at the very highest level tends to attract and recruit people who are very much like themselves. In other words, if you were to conduct the Minnesota Multiphasic Inventory (MMPI) test on the person most responsible for recruiting new lawyers in a large law firm, the lawyers she recruits would probably be uncannily similar to her in the MMPI profile. And she would probably have a profile similar to the lawyer who recruited her…and on and on up and down the lawyer line.

It is easy to recognize that law firms huge and small take on the qualities, good and bad, of the leadership within the organization. It really does all flow from the top. The priorities, character, and decency or lack of decency most of the time are developed by the leadership within a firm in such a way that the entire firm adopts most of the good and most of the bad from that leadership.

According to Sol Linowitz, author of *The Betrayed Profession,* there is more at risk than our individual undeveloped spirituality when we allow the spiritually blind to hire and lead the spiritually blind. Linowitz says the end result is as follows:

> The associates in the large firms cannot play the piano or paint a picture or act in a church play because they simply don't have the time. The tragedy is that, in the end, the single-minded drive toward winning the competitions at the firm will make these young lawyers not only less useful citizens, less interesting human beings, and less successful parents but also less good as lawyers, less sympathetic to other people's troubles, and less valuable to their clients.

❧

Chapter Three
Seeing

THERE WAS A MAN *who spent a huge amount of his time studying the stars. He believed he could see the future by observing the movement of the stars.*

He would walk the streets around his beautiful village home with his eyes fixed entirely, completely, on the night sky as he looked for this or that special star. His eyes were always fixed on the beautiful stars above.

As he was walking and stargazing one night, he fell into a pit that he had failed to notice.

Several people who lived in the beautiful little village heard the man crying for help and came to his assistance. As they pulled the man out of the pit, one of his n e i g h b o r s pointed out that the man had spent so much time gazing at the stars that he often failed to notice or pay attention to all the other parts of the world around him.

In Figueles, in the Catalonia Region of Spain, there is a museum that was built by Salvador Dali as a gift to the people of his hometown and to house many of his important works. At the museum's grand entranceway, you are immediately confronted with the challenge of seeing what Dali saw and of observing what Dali observed about the world. You are challenged to identify the image of Abraham Lincoln within a huge canvas covered with a rainbow of paints, a collection of painted squares, cubes, abstract shapes. The museum guide tells you to stand back as far as possible and slightly squint your eyes. He suggests that you turn your head a bit and rely on peripheral vision to identify the portrait of the sixteenth president of the United States. Eventually, the guide explains to you that generally half of the people confronted with this challenge actually see the head of Lincoln and appreciate the image. Another 25 percent profess to see Lincoln when they really don't, and still another 25 percent become frustrated to the point that they move on to the next room, dismissing the genius of Dali as nothing more than meaningless, abstract nonsense. In other words, according to the museum guide, about half the observers, when confronted with one of Dali's most important works, simply "don't know how to see." Somewhere along the way, they have cluttered their minds so completely with things that never require any art or method of observation that the basic skill is eventually lost, and they forget how to really see what is around them.

If We Can't Eat It, We Don't See It.

Author James Atkins is an art historian who has devoted much of his life to helping art students remember how to see. In Atkins' book *The Object Stares Back,* he explains that we forget how to see because the process is completely "entangled in passions of jealousy, possessiveness, and is soaked in affect—in pleasure and displeasure." He suggests that the art of seeing is not simply a function of pointing our eyes at a particular scene or object and creating an imprint on our retina. We must first understand how our life experiences affect what we see and help dictate what we don't see. For example, sociologists and psychologists tell us that what occupies our mind and actions most of our time day to day is the act of survival. Most of our time is devoted to thinking about hunting and gathering. Therefore, we train ourselves to observe the world as hunters and gatherers. Like the stargazer in Aesop's fable, we become single-minded about the things on which we focus.

Pulitzer Prize–winning author Annie Dillard, in her book *Pilgrim at Tinker Creek,* concludes that seeing is a "discipline requiring a lifetime of dedicated struggles." She points out that one important step is to overcome, to "hush the noise of useless interior babble" that keeps us from seeing, much like a newspaper dangled in front of our eyes. Overcoming the minutiae that monopolize our time and attention as lawyers requires a tremendous desire. It requires a desire that is greater than our need to always be in control of every phone call, every personal interaction, every event that takes place in our law office each day, every unnecessary obligation that further and further dulls our sense of vision to the point that we grow accustomed to only selectively seeing the world around us each day. Striving to selectively see the world, focusing all the power of our eyesight on only one thing has harmful side-effects. Peter Freuchen describes how too much strain of selectively *seeing* can create sickness in human beings. Dillard quotes Freuchen in her essay on *seeing:*

> The Greenland fjords are peculiar for the spells of completely quiet weather, when there is not enough wind to blow out a match and the water is like a sheet of glass. The kayak hunter must sit in his boat without stirring a finger so as not to scare the shy seals away....The sun, low in the sky, sends a glare into his eyes, and the landscape around moves into the realm of the unreal. The reflection from the mirror-like water hypnotizes him, he seems to be unable to move, and all of a sudden it is as if he were floating in a bottomless void, sinking, sinking, and sinking....Horror-stricken, he tries to stir, to cry out, but he cannot, he is completely paralyzed, he just falls and falls.

Dillard adds that some of the most skilled and accomplished hunters become so handicapped by this selective seeing sickness that they often "bring ruin and sometimes starvation to their families."

Dillard could just as easily have used descriptions of the many sinking, paralyzed hunting and gathering lawyers as a teaching example to make her point. There are many of us who have been staring without interruption at the things that we believe will enable us to feed our family. Hunting and gathering has become our single focus because the overwhelming majority of lawyers within our ranks do not believe they have enough.

For example, in a questionnaire that was designed to explore topics discussed in this book, 76 percent of the respondents said that they are not at the point in their career when they have enough financial wealth to allow themselves to enjoy life. Attitudes like that put us in the same posture as the seal hunter sitting in a kayak, spear raised, eyes fixed, unable to observe any other parts of the world around us. We fall into the very type of hole Aesop warned us about because we lose the knack of effectively scanning all parts of the world around us.

The Wisdom of Not Waiting to See

Author Robert Hastings, in his short essay "The Station," does a good job of describing the illness that develops in far too many of us when we spend a lifetime conditioning ourselves not to look up until we have maneuvered ourselves to some mystical place that allows us to at last enjoy our surroundings:

Tucked away in our subconscious is an idyllic vision. We see ourselves on a long trip that spans the continent. We are traveling by train. Out the windows we drink in the passing scene of cars on nearby highways, of children waving at a crossing, of cattle grazing on a distant hillside, of smoke pouring from a power plant, of row upon row of corn and wheat, of flat lands and valleys, of mountains and rolling hillsides, of city skylines and village halls.

But uppermost in our minds is the final destination. Bands will be playing and flags waving. Once we get there, our dreams will come true, and the pieces of our lives will fit together like a jigsaw puzzle. How restlessly we pace the aisles, damning the minutes for loitering— waiting, waiting, waiting for the station.

"When we reach the station, that will be it!" we cry.

"When I'm 18."

"When I buy a new 450SL Mercedes-Benz!"

"When I put the last kid through college."

"When I have paid off the mortgage!"

"When I get a promotion."

"When I reach the age of retirement, I shall live happily ever after!"

Sooner or later, we must realize there is no station, no one place to arrive at once and for all. The true joy of life is the trip. The station is only a dream. It constantly outdistances us.

Hastings is restating what we have heard so many times but usually are unwilling to believe. He is telling us that our ability to see, acknowledge, and appreciate all that we have been blessed with seldom improves as the number, quality, and frequency of those blessings continue to grow. We can't see those blessings, much less appreciate them, because our eyes are fixed too far down the road at the next "station"…or perhaps the next or the next. We have trained ourselves to believe that it is that moment far down the road that we will finally see and appreciate as being that "perfect moment" when people and events line up exactly the way we expect; then we can stop to see and appreciate—maybe even be grateful.

In the meantime, too much of the world around us remains hidden, barely noticeable to untrained eyes. Bill Baker has practiced law more than eighteen years. He recounts this experience:

> I spent about a week in Key West taking depositions one summer. There is a place in that town along the pier at the end of a street named Duval where people almost every day gather to watch the sun set. I had gone to Key West not to watch sunsets but to take

depositions. But each day one person or

another in that town would ask me, "Did you

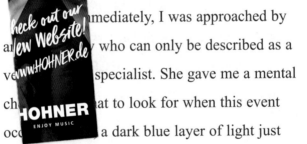

set yesterday?"

felt a little dull and maybe even a

when I would make up some lame

ot having taken the time to see

So one day, I did. Still buttoned up

iece suit, briefcase in hand, I

r this event.

mediately, I was approached by

who can only be described as a

specialist. She gave me a mental

at to look for when this event

a dark blue layer of light just

above the horizon as the sun begins to settle

into the water. Then a flash of radiant orange-

purple beams of light appears just above the

top of the water along both sides of the sun.

Then, the water as far as the eye can see turns

an almost phosphorescent green. Then, finally,

as the sun sinks below the water, below the horizon, one last thin column of orange light shoots straight up, barely above the water, and just above where the sun used to be.

As I watched, I actually saw some of what she told me I would see. I was the only one laughing in the crowd as the event came to an end. My laughter caught the attention of many of the watchers standing around me. I wanted to tell them what I was laughing about. I wanted to let them know that I was laughing at myself because I did see that last column of orange light exploding over the top of that incredibly beautiful setting sun. I wanted to let them know how awkward I felt that it was the first time I had watched a sunset since the time I started law school fifteen years before.

An Artist's Technique for Seeing

I remember sitting on the observation deck of a cruise ship as it pulled out of the port of Cozumel, Mexico, late one April afternoon. Some aspects of what I observed were overwhelmingly obvious. The water was almost cobalt, and, yes, the sky was clear to the point that visibility was limitless and, yes, there was a brisk breeze that was borderline chilly. But as I sat there noticing the obvious, I asked my wife what an artist would see that I was unable to see. How would an artist express this experience in a way that I was unable to express?

She gave me the type of logical, commonsense answer that I have grown accustomed to hearing throughout the many years of our marriage. She said two things. Number one: Artists have trained themselves to see what we so often overlook. Number two: They "allow" themselves to see what we constantly seem to overlook.

Okay. The first part of what she said was good news to me because it indicated that she believed there is probably a methodology for observing. And if there was such a methodology, I could surely figure it out. The second part, however, was troubling, and I am certain she meant for it to be troubling in a kind way. Although she said that artists "allow" themselves to see what *we* constantly seem to overlook, her preference would have been to replace the word "we" with the word "you." No matter, she didn't need to say it.

When my wife said artists *allow* themselves to see what others overlook, I clearly understood her meaning. She was reminding me that, like so many people who lawyer for a living, I more often than not observe the world around me on a "need to know," a "need to see," a "need to hear" basis and overlook so much of what I believe I don't need to know, don't need to observe, don't need to hear! Too often, a logic-oriented, analytical, calculating type of looking and listening overcomes any introspective type of observation I ought to be capable of. I place importance in a method of seeing and observing that helps me pay my bills—a hunter-gatherer way of seeing.

For example, I have pretty well adapted to the act of observing the nuances or the mannerisms of an expert witness. During my cross-examination of that witness, I am tuned in to his speech cadence, his body language, his syntax. I listen even for what he doesn't say. I sense the slightest chink in his armor because I not only *allow* myself to make those observations, I demand it of myself. But my wife's point was that I don't discipline myself and I don't allow myself to so keenly observe the rest of the world around me. Many good lawyer friends that I have shared this thought with tell me that I am not alone in my inability to keenly and creatively observe the world in a way that is broader, a way that is more than simply expedient.

So what would a trained professional artist have seen as we pulled away from the coastline in Cozumel that afternoon? What would she have been trained to look for in observing that small slice of the world?

The Method of Seeing What an Artist Sees

A friend of mine who makes her living as a professional artist answered the question I had about differences in how I observed the coast of Cozumel and what she might see in that same spectacular vista. She began explaining those differences by stating that we all think in terms of images and pictures. In other words, as you sit reading the words on this page, you are analyzing the content of those words by formulating hundreds, maybe even thousands, of pictures and images for your brain to process. Your brain is attempting to help itself efficiently operate by converting words and simple ideas into pictures.

Our life experience to a large degree helps us add dimension, spatial relationship, light, color, and depth. For example, if a person reading the words on this page is thinking about a Cozumel coast, the pictures that he is formulating may have more detail and color if he has seen the Cozumel coast at some point in his life. His life experience actually primes and promotes his ability to add texture and depth to that scene as the picture flashes through his brain in less than a millisecond. You might even say there is a direct relationship between the quality of that picture and the quality of his life. The quality of both are tightly intertwined.

Artists who are serious about their art and trade understand that relationship. Claude Monet could project onto canvas the beauty of the sunlight's effect on the valley of the Creuse because his life experience enabled him to actually see more color, more texture, more quality than the typical non-artist.

But more importantly, when Monet saw or heard words that included mention of that valley, his mental pictures were substantially more vibrant and detailed because he had spent a lifetime training himself to see 10 shades of red or 12 shades of blue, and he had, after all, actually visited that valley.

In a delicate, diplomatic way, I believe my artistic friend was telling me that, because she has paid attention to color shades, perspective, and dimensions almost every day of her life (and I have not), *(a)* she could soak up more of the beauty that Cozumel coast had to offer as the ship pulled away, and *(b)* the spoken or written words describing that coast might cause her to visualize a more detailed, maybe even more colorful picture than the one that would struggle to take form in my mind.

In our role as lawyers, the overwhelming majority of the words we read don't cause us to conjure up mental pictures of a peaceful-looking Mexican coast or spectacular-looking French valleys. Most of the words we hear, read, and write are combative, confrontational, competitive, hostile, and severe. We expose ourselves to those types of mental pictures and imagery at least five days a week for an average of 32 years.

The words that we are exposed to every day don't cause us to visualize pictures with bright colors, creative dimension, or interesting perspective. In fact, they are words that dull our sense for visualizing such things.

According to what this talented artist was explaining to me, it is that dulling of our senses that sometimes obscures our imagination and artistic vision. Worse yet, after years of disuse, the part of our brain that helps us look at our world with creativity and artistic insight edges toward becoming dysfunctional.

In a matter-of-fact way, this woman who makes her living as a professional artist explained how artists see by giving me a basic refresher course in the physiology of the brain. She explained that the human brain is divided into a right hemisphere and a left hemisphere for a reason. The right and left sides act independently of one another, giving us what is often referred to as "two minds." Those two symmetrical lobes also balance the symmetry of opposites, the right side being creative and the left side being analytical and logical. If you live too much by use of the left mind, you can forget how to use your right mind because your two minds naturally oppose each other.

She went on to explain that the left side is the verbal side, and the right side is mute. The right hemisphere of the brain enables us to understand metaphors. It allows us to dream and create new combinations of ideas. The left hemisphere, on the other hand, permits us to analyze, abstract, count, plan time, and make rational statements based on logic. With our left brain we gather data, and with our right brain we creatively transfer that data: we apply an artistic vision to that data.

There were a few other points she made about the right brain that seem important in understanding the differences between her artist eyes and my lawyer eyes. They are that the right brain is nonrational, willing to suspend judgment. It is intuitive: it makes leaps of insight often based on incomplete patterns, undefined space, and vague dimensions. It is holistic: it sees and shapes all things at once as opposed to the way the linear left brain functions.

Obviously, the right side of my brain was not highly developed enough to appreciate everything I should have appreciated about that Cozumel coast.

That talented artist, who has been kind enough to create three book jackets for me, including the one on this book, explained a few things to me about seeing. I was able to conclude that when all parts of that grey matter between my ears are operating properly, I see the world more completely.

The Cozumel coast scenery becomes inseparable from the experience of the breeze upon your face, the sunlight on your skin, the reflections on the water, the sound of the waves against the ship, the lilting movement of the vessel, and your displaced sense of being in an unfamiliar, stimulating place. Relaxing and taking in the moment nonjudgmentally, *receiving* the moment and *being* in the moment, you see through the eyes of an artist.

As I listened, I actually caught my right hand easing its way up to the side of my head to see if I had developed a concavity on the right side of my skull. I was certain that after eighteen years of lawyering, I had lost more than a moderate amount of grey matter on that side of my brain. It even occurred to me that I had developed the same type of dull barbarian brain that is from time to time associated with the qualities of the successful modern lawyer.

An article appeared in the *American University Law Review* in 1997. The author, Susan Daicoff, undertook the tedious job of putting together empirical data that shed some light on the typical character profile of the modern lawyer. She cites a handful of impressive-looking studies where a few conclusions about lawyer personality traits are consistent. One of those conclusions is that lawyers have personality traits that cause them to be less philosophical and introspective and more impersonal, calculating, and logic oriented than the normal population. The author of one of the studies Daicoff cited chose to use more direct words to describe lawyers, saying that we are "colder" and less "affiliative" than normal people.

In fact, one study discussed in Daicoff's article concluded that the law student who placed too much value in relationships with people did not fare well in law school. Another quality that was a liability for a law student according to the same study was an overuse of "feeling-oriented" decision making as opposed to more calculated, logical, impersonal "thinking-oriented" decision making. The law student with this suspect personality trait of "feeling-oriented" decision making had a dropout rate about four times as high as his better-adjusted law school buddies.

It is difficult to read Daicoff's article without conjuring up images of the Indian savage's failures and shortcomings among a "brave new world" of Alpha Plus Intellectuals. One of Aldous Huxley's themes for his 1932 science fiction novel about a perfectly ordered but dehumanized culture was that a lack of introspective, creative, observation and thinking—a lack of a "feeling-oriented" way of seeing the world—dooms that culture to failure. Huxley wanted his readers to appreciate the contrast between the savage's constant observation of his surroundings, both things and people, and the highly evolved Alpha Plus Intellectuals' failure to see.

He wanted to make the point that the savage had the greater capacity for seeing colors, shapes, and textures. The savage had a more refined ability to hear sounds and to actually hear and understand what people around him were asking of him and telling him. Most important, though, was Huxley's point that the savage was superbly equipped to show the type of sensitivity, compassion, and emotions that humanized his relationships with people. The Alpha Plus Intellectuals' interactions with people were motivated not by the good qualities they actually saw in other people but by what they wanted to extract from those people.

There are a few similarities between the "highly evolved" vision of Huxley's Alpha Plus Intellectuals and the type of vision lawyers begin to refine the day they start law school. That "refined" vision causes us more than our share of problems:

> My first marriage lasted a little more than
> five years. That marriage came at a bad time.
> We were two young attorneys with our eyes
> fixed on a career that demanded unwavering
> focus, uncompromising and undivided
> attention. We were the proverbial two ships
> passing in the night. We often talked about the
> hours we worked, the sacrifices we made as if

there was something noble and honorable about what we gave up to be the best and most successful lawyers we could be. Even when we did have time together, it was as if we only saw each other with a distracted, partial, almost peripheral vision that never allowed either one of us much insight into what was going on in the other's life. The truth is that I am not certain either one of us placed much importance on such insight. The way we looked at each other during the last year of that marriage can only be described as selfish and ungiving, almost like two strangers looking over the tops of each other's head to see who else or what else took up space within our line of sight.

Our spouses, children, family, and friends should register as more than an unfocused imprint upon our retinas. If Annie Dillard is correct that seeing is a "discipline requiring a lifetime of dedicated struggle," then we should dedicate most of that effort to not just glancing daily at our children as they enter and exit our homes, not just noticing our spouse from time to time with our peripheral vision, but really *seeing* these people with a focused, disciplined, trained eye.

How many times have we heard a client, friend, or colleague tell us about some awful event that occurred with their children or their spouse? Something their child did that they didn't understand. Something they usually described as an event they "never saw coming." If seeing is hard work, if it requires "dedicated struggle," then we need to dedicate at least as much effort to our family and friends as we do to recognizing our prey as we hunt and gather.

To See with Feeling

Elihu Root was a Nobel Peace Prize–winner who lawyered during the early 1900s. He lived 92 years, and during that time his accomplishments as a legal ethicist, as a statesman, and as a social philosopher were monumental.

Root was busier and pulled in more directions than the typical lawyer, but his disciplined vision, his focused sight that fixed on family, friends, and business associates, was remarkably different from the sight of the lawyer who is simply a hunter and gatherer.

Root apparently had a habit of staring at friends and associates without speaking a word for uncomfortably long periods of time. He would sit and simply observe people with an almost starry-eyed expression, quietly watching while others in a room were quick to speak. Root would thoughtfully observe the people who were caught up in the hustle of the crisis of the day or the moment. He would observe; he would see people the same way that we might observe or see a sunset: with trained eyes, with disciplined eyes, with eyes that were focused by the desire to *really see* family, friends, and even associates, not as a hunter and gatherer might see them, but as one compassionate human being trying to understand and appreciate another.

One cost to not seeing properly is a cost that is often passed on to the people who mean the most to us in our lives. It is a cost that is typically passed on to our family and friends. As we fix our "need-to-know" vision on the most minute details of lawyering, we fail to take enough notice of people in our lives who become nothing short of blind spots.

In the late 1800s, Elihu Root scheduled a trip to Europe for himself and his brother. It was a trip that

Root scheduled during his busiest time as a lawyer. His life as a lawyer during this period was no less complicated and stressed than that of any attorney reading the words on this page. He was at the height of his hunting and gathering routine. But his vision had not deteriorated to the point that he failed to see and appreciate the beauty of relationships with his family and friends. He scheduled his trip to Europe because his brother was dying of tuberculosis and he wanted to be with him. He wanted to help him get well if possible, knowing full well that at that time there was no cure for his brother's disease.

This was not a vacation for Root. Under the best conditions, a trip abroad in 1870 was no picnic, and making the trip with a dying brother who had to be carried upstairs and from place to place must have been a sad and horrible experience of Elihu Root. The trip did not save his brother's life, and the long journey left Root almost in financial ruin. Root made that trip because, after many years of practicing law, he had managed not to become handicapped with the type of selective seeing that so often brings ruin to our relationships with family and friends. In 1870, Root could "see" his brother. He combined his ability to feel compassion and empathy with his ability to observe his brother's predicament. Root's vision was clear enough to understand that there was no commitment, obligation, responsibility, or expectation that carried more weight than this member of his family, this friend, this human being, who desperately needed to be not merely noticed, but actually seen and valued by Root.

Researchers such as Connie Beck, Bruce Sales, and Andrew Benjamin are a few of the handful of researchers who have designed and performed psychological profile testing focusing specifically on lawyers' lives. Their studies emphasized the importance of lawyers' relearning to see family and friends with the same type of feelings and clarity so often exhibited by Elihu Root as he interacted with people.

Those studies tell us that, in the opinion of the researchers, there exists an "impending crisis for lawyers' family lives." The studies, drawing on empirical data, tell us that lawyers who are working more, reducing vacation time, and spending less time with family members are jeopardizing their lives and the lives of the people they profess to care about the most.

The findings of the Beck, Sales, and Benjamin studies are painfully clear: both male and female lawyers are doing a very poor job of fostering sustainable, feeling, sensitive, affectionate relationships.

Lawyers are not placing a significant amount of importance in the process of even talking and interacting with the important people in their lives. How then can we expect to ever really see our children, our spouses, and friends with the same type of feeling, refined, compassionate vision that Elihu Root showed his brother?

According to the Beck studies, female lawyers are doing even worse than their male coworkers in developing and maintaining happy and fulfilling significant relationships. Just like male lawyers, they are willing to spend hours, days, weeks, months, and years trying to please clients, senior partners, and professional peers all the while they are allowing their ability to see and perhaps even fuel the emotional needs of family and friends to atrophy.

Learning to See Ourselves

I was invited to speak at a continuing legal education seminar in Rochester, New York. It was an impressive group of attorneys. Most of the people attending that seminar would probably be characterized as the leadership of that moderately large bar association.

The organizer of that program had called me the week before the program was to take place to emphasize to me that he wanted me during that three-hour program to discuss issues that are not typically part of a C.L.E. program. He wanted the focus of this program to be appreciably different from the typical bar-related seminar. He explained that he had a hope that my presentation and the panel discussion that would follow would encourage the attendees to take a critical look at their lives as lawyers.

He did not want a "we can do better" speech. He did not want a speech that focused on what a wonderful profession lawyering had the potential to become. He wanted a three-hour presentation that would promote a process of self-perception for the room full of lawyers attending that seminar. The type of self-perception that requires us to see ourselves with more honesty, humility, and open-mindedness than we take the time to apply on most days when we hold ourselves out as legal and life counselors to other people.

The list of topics I incorporated into my presentation that day included greed, dishonesty, unhealthy ego, blind ambition, lack of courage, lack of character, and their impact on lawyering. I was certain my discussion of those topics would push the envelope on criticism of our profession. I suspected that this room full of bar leaders in that Rochester area would have all the self-perception their well-trained ears would want to hear about after 30 minutes or so of my unkinder and ungentler presentation.

In that first 30 minutes, there was an ample amount of squirming, an abundance of nervous coughs, and even a few nervous giggles, but there was no thin skin in that room. As the program progressed, it was clear that they wanted to hear more. They wanted to think more about topics that certainly had to push their limits of humility and open-mindedness.

If any one of those lawyers was offended that day, no one ever let me know about it. In fact, the group discussions that took place among all the attendees in the last hour of the program made it clear that not only were they not offended by the hard jagged edges to the topics presented, they wanted to hear more.

The dynamics of what was taking place in that room that day would not have surprised a good sociologist as much as it surprised me, because a trained sociologist would have understood that most people in this world have an unfathomable desire to *see themselves* as the rest of the world might see them.

Mankind has been challenged with the idea of answering the question of "who, what, and why am I" since the first caveman began drawing stick figures on the walls of whatever cave he called home.

The lawyers in that room that day were driven by that same unshakable desire. They wanted to see themselves more clearly in hopes of better understanding who they are—what they look like to the rest of the world.

When we are shown group pictures that include us, we will search for our own "unique," "special" face in that group shot before our eyes are drawn to any other part of the photograph. Because no matter how many years we have lived with ourselves, we are always trying to gain a closer picture of ourselves for ourselves. We are drawn to the idea of creating a sustainable image of who we are, what we are, and how we appear and are regarded by other people.

Some of us are more skillful than others when it comes to seeing ourselves with any accurate detail. Those people with the greater skill in seeing themselves as they really are, are happier, more content, and more peaceful people according to the empirical data that modern sociologists have to share with us.

According to the survey that was conducted for this book:

- Sixty-seven percent of the respondents believed that the more successful they *appeared* to be, the more business they would get as a lawyer.
- Fifty percent of the respondents said that they are a member of at least one organization not because they enjoy it, but because it is good for their career.
- Eighty-nine percent said that in their opinion

113

lawyers' overspending beyond their financial ability has become a self-destructive behavior within our profession.

It is difficult to build our skills of accurately seeing ourselves when we surround ourselves with so much smoke and so many mirrors. The smoke and mirrors result in clever barrier building between who and what we really are and the images we are attempting to portray for the rest of the world. Those barriers make it unlikely that we will ever really see or know ourselves with much accuracy. The "lawyer" we are portraying generally is far from being the "person" that we are.

When the world's greatest philosophers began asking "who am I" about 1500 B.C., they asked the questions not because they imagined it was good material for self-help books, but because they believed that a civilization improves itself if the leadership of that civilization can learn how to better see themselves. Those philosophers regarded really seeing and knowing oneself as a skill that could be learned and improved.

Philosophers such as Aesop have always worked diligently to expose the dangers of self-avoidance.

They have urged us to overcome our tendency to resist accurately knowing or seeing ourselves. They have tried to explain the pitfalls of never thinking deeply…never thinking with an open mind about who or what we really are.

Aesop delivered his admonition this way:

One day, a leopard was arguing with a wise old fox about who had the most attractive appearance. The leopard took great pride in his colorful spotted coat and pointed out to the wise old fox that the fox's coat was boring, common, and unexceptional in every regard.

The fox did not need to hear from the leopard that his appearance was inferior to the leopard's. In fact, he was well aware of that. He had long known and accepted the strengths and weaknesses of his appearance. However, the fox also understood that his strength lay in his wisdom and wit. He exercised that wisdom and wit by goading the leopard about his shortcomings in hopes of forcing the leopard to see beyond his spotted, shiny coat. In fact, just as the leopard was about to lose his temper over the fox's goading, the fox began to make his exit. With his parting shot, he told the leopard that, yes, the leopard did have the finer appearance, but what he had in the way of wisdom would always be lacking because of that fine coat.

The type of self-appraisal or self-perception that the fox was goading the leopard to engage in is the same type of self-appraisal that lawyers should openly embrace. The overwhelming majority of us still make our living as counselors of people. Those people we counsel benefit when we force ourselves to understand what really lies below our well-groomed shiny coat. They benefit when we make consistent efforts to better know ourselves, to know whether we have a mean, dishonest, envious, manipulative, jealous, greedy, spirit. Aren't we better counselors when we admit to those shortcomings and then every day attempt to lessen the negative impact those poor qualities have on our lives and the lives of our clients, family, co-workers, and friends? When we deny the existence of those unattractive character traits, we fail to use any energy whatsoever to control the harm those impulses invariably cause.

Every now and then, purely by accident, we are able to gain an insight about what lies below our colorful, shiny coats. Most of the time, we do not plan, expect, or even desire to learn about a character trait in ourselves that surfaces and causes us shock and dismay. The most extreme undesirable character traits reveal themselves to us very sparingly. For 20 years, we may live with a character trait that, when reduced to writing or spoken word, looks and sounds cheesy and unattractive by anyone's standards.

For example, for 20 years, we may have lived with a manipulative tendency that results in a ceaseless effort to extract from family, friends, and the world at large every ounce of anything that benefits our selfish needs.

Or perhaps we find it pleasing to see other people fail even when their failure has no impact on our lives, positive or negative.

Those are the types of traits that the Aesops of the world have urged us to methodically uncover and reveal to ourselves. Because it is exactly those types of traits that we otherwise will only get brief glimpses of almost purely by accident from time to time throughout our lives.

It is simply too easy to live the life of the leopard, paying so much attention to the colorful, attractive image we wish to project that we avoid the attempt to bring quality to our lives by improving on substance rather than form. Escaping self-awareness will ensure less anxiety, disappointment, discomfort and disillusionment for short periods of our lives. Ignorance about ourselves, like any other ignorance, is bliss.

Avoiding the process of self-perception is inappropriate for people who are in the business of counseling parents involved in ugly custody battles, people who have lost loved ones in catastrophic accidents, or business owners who are looking for legal loopholes to justify actions that are simply dishonest.

It is not difficult to understand that there is an important relationship between how accurately we understand ourselves and the caliber of advice we give our clients. Bill Lee, a trial lawyer who has practiced for more than 20 years, describes that relationship this way:

> I have more than my share of the types of character traits that we are quick to notice and even quicker to criticize when we see them surface in other lawyers.

> I have at times regarded my inability to see myself with perfect clarity as something of a blessing. There have even been times when I

119

have wondered if knowing all the details and truths about my 48-year-old character is actually more information than I really needed to have.

But fortunately, serious life-changing events during my career as a lawyer have forced me to make a few conclusions about myself. I have concluded that when I can accurately recognize and constantly acknowledge all the warts, blots, and blemishes that make up who I really am at times, then I can begin making a few improvements. I can give advice that is not tainted by those character blots and blemishes.

The advice I give as a counselor becomes less influenced by elements of dishonesty, greed, selfishness, and pride because they don't sneak up on me. I remain aware that they always threaten to surface. They always threaten to dismantle good decision making.

Chapter Four
Addictive Ambition

THERE WAS A TIME *when the Peacock did not have the huge decorative feathers that now distinguish it from more common, less showy birds. In fact, the peacock had to plead with the gods to grant him a huge set of intricately patterned tail feathers. The peacock's ambition was to have bigger, more beautiful feathers than all the other birds so that the other birds would be envious. Once the very proud peacock's wish was granted, he* *would attract attention to what he had and what the other birds did not have by parading his iridescent tail feathers in front of the other birds.*

One day, the beautifully colored peacock noticed that an eagle was lazily soaring high above the clouds, obviously enjoying the view of the earth below. The peacock remembered what

a wonderful feeling it was to soar high above the earth—to enjoy the freedom of flight—so he began flapping his wings to fly with the eagle. It was then that he realized that those feathers that looked so beautiful—those feathers that he had so completely coveted—were preventing him from flying. Those tail feathers that he wanted the other birds to envy were now starting to resemble heavy chains that held him so close to the ground that he would never again enjoy the freedom of flight.

A response included in the questionnaire that is the appendix of this book sheds light on the fact that most of us have a poorly defined notion of what will bring us happiness.

An overwhelming majority of the respondents to that questionnaire believed that if they would defer enjoying their lives today, they could work toward a place of financial security that would at last bring them happiness. Seventy percent of the respondents either believed that they might feel financially secure 20 years from now or weren't sure they would ever feel financially secure. Seventy-six percent do not have enough right now to relax and feel content about their lives. Here are some thoughts expressed by Andy Childers, a Georgia lawyer:

I saw another one of those magazine articles recently where a handful of lawyers were bragging about the multimillions they had made as attorneys. They were posed in front of their palatial estates. They were bragging about what they owned and what they were going to buy: ships, jets, all the things that were going to make these 55- to 65-year-old lawyers happy. I can honestly say that I felt absolutely no envy as I looked at those pictures and read that article. However, as I read on, I did pause to wonder if there was some type of defect in my makeup or character as a lawyer. I wondered if I was missing some vital helix in an important DNA strand that should be pushing me to want more prestige, more power, more wealth in my life. As I read that article, I wondered if it was woefully abnormal to be a lawyer in the year 2000 who did not believe that my self-worth was gauged by the standards of those superficial images appearing on the pages of that magazine.

What Childers may have been seeing in the picture and in the copy that appeared on the pages of that magazine has been characterized by modern philosophers and sociologists as "addictive ambition." Ken Keyes, who could best be described as an important modern thinker, borrowed the wisdom of great thinkers who had gone before him in developing the concept he labeled "addictive ambition." His theory is as follows: From the time we first began as children to visualize the world around us with a rational mind, we began developing self-absorbed demands and expectations about what types of events, situations, and possessions would bring us happiness and unhappiness. After years of programming ourselves about which events, situations, or types of possessions would bring us even temporary happiness, we actually became addicted to lining the world up in a way that would satisfy those addictions.

Keyes borrowed more from philosophers than from psychologists to develop his theory that most of those addictions flow out of a desire for security and a desire for power. That security center is where our thoughts and efforts are dominated by an effort to get not only "enough" for just today or tomorrow but "enough" for 10, 20, 30 years from now. More importantly, that security center has trained itself to determine that we have "enough" only when we have more than the other guy. Likewise, our desire for power centers itself in such a way that our thoughts and efforts, our addiction to being bigger, better, to having more prestige, more power, are dominated by an effort to have enough of that not just today but 30 years from now when we will, we hope, have more than the other guy.

These addiction centers become stronger and stronger with a lifetime of very bad programming. Whenever there is a threat to one of these centers, a host of unhealthy emotions takes control of our lives. Emotions such as anger, anxiety, jealousy, resentment, and discontentment make their way to the surface of our lives and stay there a great deal of the time.

Keyes' theories center in the belief that most addictions have similar qualities and that our addiction to satisfying a sometimes unhealthy ego is similar to all our other addictions.

Most of us in the legal profession never get to the point where our security center or our power center is quieted into accepting the place in the world that we actually occupy. We are always driven by visions of the place we want someday to occupy.

The positive spin on that, of course, is to say that we are "highly motivated," that we are Type A "over-achievers." Perhaps we feel a sense of pride well up inside when we are referred to as "movers and shakers," "rainmakers," or "deal makers," maybe even "masters of the game."

According to the experts, the most difficult step in confronting and taming most addictions is the acknowledgment that an addiction actually exists. Ninety-seven percent of the lawyers who answered the questionnaire included as an appendix in this book agreed with the statement: "I believe that ambition within our profession does have the potential to take on an addictive nature." And 88 percent agreed that "I have known people in the lawyering profession whose ambitions I would consider equivalent to an addiction."

But of the respondents who were willing to label their *peers* as ambition addicts, 60 percent said that *they* don't worry about financial success as much as *other lawyers* do. Also, almost 80 percent of the lawyers who perceived a problem with addictive ambition among other lawyers said that *they* don't place unrealistic expectations on *their* lawyering career.

So who are these "other lawyers," these ambition addicts, these other people who are our professional peers, this other group of lawyers among us who are not as well adjusted as the rest of us? More importantly, how is their addictive nature affecting *their* lives and fortunately not *ours*?

When we take a less positive and less flattering spin on what the "highly motivated," "overachieving" lawyers are doing to their lives these days, we would need to include at least a few of the following personality traits that often surface:

- Most of the time they are willing to defer enjoyment of the possessions they now have while they work toward obtaining more or bigger possessions such as homes, vacation homes, boats, etc.

- They cannot feel content about their sense of achievement until their family, friends, and professional peers, acknowledge that achievement—until they receive clear, unequivocal recognition for those accomplishments.

- Once they excel by completing one impressive accomplishment or achievement, they mentally raise their expectations of what they have to achieve or accomplish next. There is always an obsession to advance their definition of meaningful achievement or accomplishment.

- They continually feel uneasy about their lives until events, friends, and even family members line up in such a way that they feel they are finally "in control of" all these things.

- They seldom have a clearly defined mental picture of what is "enough."

- Most of the time, they are working toward a point in their lives when they believe they will not have to answer to any higher authority—a time when they can conduct their lives with complete autonomy— perhaps even a time when they are secure and powerful enough to snub or ignore the rest of the world because they will at last be in total control of their lives.

- They have a tendency to build artificial walls and barriers as they addictively hunt and gather. They are afraid to even experiment with living a life on the other side of those walls that they have built for themselves. Those walls, in their minds, bring order, structure, and relevance to their ambition.

- They often lose sight of the intrinsic value of many aspects of life that do not pay a financial dividend—aspects of life that do not have a dollar benefit but nevertheless improve the overall quality of our lives, such as friendship, family, or maybe learning something new merely for the satisfaction of learning. They arrive at a point where virtually every activity in their lives is in some way associated with gaining more control, more security, more power. All things begin to be categorized in order of importance, almost by dollar value.

- Their day-to-day living is guided by an unshakable *me versus them* attitude as they compete for a bigger share of security and power. That attitude enables them to begin treating more people they come in contact with as merely a means to an end.

If we were advising our most important clients about how to bring more joy and happiness into their lives, we could no doubt begin by having them abandon all of the qualities listed above.

If we identified such characteristics in our children, how would we advise them? I asked Larry Morris, a lawyer who has practiced more than twenty years to give the topic some thought. Here is what he wrote;

I have three children ranging in age from 11 to 18. Like any parent, I have learned a lot about *myself* as I have watched them mature. I remember watching the demeanor of my son as a four-year-old, often going from joy to jealousy because he could not hoard more toys than his playmates. I have watched my daughters turn moody and almost maudlin over minor failures, failures that caused them to doubt their position of influence and prestige among their other teenage friends.

When I admonished and instructed my four-year-old that he could enjoy only one toy at a time, the words I spoke to him always made sense to me. When I attempted to comfort my teenage daughters by reminding that all was well in their lives even without a particular award, recognition, or accolade, my reminders always seemed like healthy, sound advice.

However, as my children have matured over the years, they have watched me as I have occasionally failed to follow the "good advice" I gave them as toddlers and young teenagers. I have lawyered for more than 20 years. I counsel people about how they should improve their lives. I know better, but I still sometimes judge my level of joy, contentment, security, and self-worth according to how many toys I have, or how much praise and recognition I can garner for myself. If I am not careful, I forget the real source of my joy and peace.

A great many of the trendy consumer shrinks of the '80s and '90s have built an entire industry selling 200-page paperbacks, videos, audio tapes, posters, and calendars that tell us that "we deserve to be in control," "we will feel better when we look out for number one," "self-centeredness is healthy," and "it is healthy to want more and to take more."

They sell their hedonistic message as if it were an official stamp of approval of the idea that "greed is good," "more is better," "I am the center of the universe," and "I deserve to have more than the other guy." It is as if they have locked arms with Madison Avenue to promote and perpetuate a "more for me" culture of consumerism. Lawyers are too willing to believe that message.

C. S. Lewis analyzed the problem this way:

Pride gets no pleasure out of having something, only out of having more of it than the next man. We say that people are proud of being rich or clever, or better-looking than others. If everyone else became equally rich, or clever, or good-looking, there would be nothing to be proud about. It is the comparison that makes you proud, the pleasure of being above the rest. Once the element of competition has gone, pride has gone.

Among lawyers who gave their opinions on the topics covered by Appendix A there was an overwhelming perception that many of their fellow attorneys have allowed their unhealthy egos to do damage to our profession. More than 75 percent of the respondents felt that was the case. Another 52 percent said that they would characterize the majority of lawyers they know as being overly self-centered. However, 71 percent felt that *they* had a "completely healthy ego." Again, it is this *other* group of attorneys that seem to be the problem.

It is not only the consumer psychologists telling us that a strong ambition for having more for ourselves is a key to happiness: self-centered ambition has been characterized as a virtue by modern philosophers such as Ayn Rand. Between 1982, the year of Rand's death, and the mid-1990s, her philosophy of objectivism gained popular appeal. Her books such as *The Fountainhead* and *The Virtue of Selfishness* told us that objectivism meant that we "must work for [our] rational self-interest with achievement of [our] own happiness as the highest moral purpose of life."

Rand's heroic characters typically are driven to have more. Having more, in fact, is what leads Rand's odd heroes to their place of "the highest moral purpose of life." They are guided by a philosophy of selfishness and greed. They are always in the process of owning "enough" of the material world regardless of the cost to family, friends, acquaintances, and competitors, regardless of how they are regarded by other occupants of this world. The unhealthy ego that Keyes says drives addictive ambition Rand regarded as positive and healthy.

Rand is certainly not the only writer or commentator willing to praise the type of self-centered ambition that begins looking an awful lot like ugly greed. In 1990, John Stossel, a news commentator, produced an entire news special for ABC in which he advocated the need for more greed in America. Viewers watching this almost surreal presentation by Stossel surely must have felt a need to turn up the volume on their television sets to make sure they were actually hearing what this shallow commentator was telling his viewers. It was the type of program where you might watch and wait thinking, *Okay, when is the punch line coming? When is this compassionless character going to tell us he is just joking?*

But there was no punch line; there was no comic relief. He was a true believer, willing to stand behind that "Greed is good." Stossel explained how the conspicuous consumption of American "robber barons" was good for all Americans. The hour-long program was an almost giddy attempt to put a warm and fuzzy edge around greed and avarice in the American culture.

Unfortunately, the program was over before Stossel was able to mention the first word about a need for business ethics or a need for balance between greed and morality. Anyone wanting to believe in the message of that program could have identified new rationales for the idea that self-indulgent conspicuous consumption leads us all to better personal well-being and social fulfillment. Stossel actually succeeded in further dumbing down the same objectivist philosophy that Rand had at least reduced to relevant literature decades before ABC aired its program. That philosophy is that selfishness, self-interest, self-centeredness, self-indulgence, egocentricism are good for you and the society you are a part of.

The "robber barons" that Stossel *idealized* in his news report and the types of heroes that Ayn Rand created in her peculiar fiction have a host of qualities that are virtually impossible to blend into the lives we have chosen as lawyers.

For example, many of us had the chance to be the Carl Icahns, the Ivan Boeskys, the Michael Milkins of the world. Their game of profiteering never required more intellect, tenacity, or commitment than most lawyers apply to their practice every day. Most of us had all the qualities necessary to be the "barbarians at the gate." But we chose not to be. I believe we chose not to be because most of us are built dramatically differently from Rand's and Stossel's heroes.

We chose another path for our lives because, *believe it or not,* most lawyers truly have a desire to serve others more than themselves. Earlier in this book, I pointed out that if you were to make a list of reasons you chose to become a lawyer, somewhere at the very top of the list would be that you wanted to claim a sense of autonomy in your life. However, also nestled somewhere in the top three reasons would be that you have a desire to serve other people in some significant way. In the last eight years, I have had the opportunity to ask dozens of lawyer groups ranging from 100 to 300 in number to create such lists, and the "desire to serve" response appears in the top three reasons as predictably as a Swiss train.

This is not one of those feel-good books written to put the best spin on the problems that haunt our profession. It certainly was not written to be "chicken soup for our souls." But the facts are what they are. The majority of us want to do good by other people, or at least we did at the time we decided to become lawyers.

The good news is that you can put silk stockings and three-piece suits on us, you can place an expensive briefcase in our hand, and most of us still have a strong desire to "serve others," to "contribute to society," to "make our world a better place to live," to "improve the quality of our world, " to "have a positive impact on people's lives." We will still put such statements in our list of reasons for wanting to become lawyers.

And we can satisfy both our desire to serve others and our need to have more security, influence, and control in the world that we serve. It is reasonable to allow a healthy ego to lead us to being a better servant, to finding a healthy, comfortable level of security, to having healthy control in our interaction with the rest of the world. However, it is next to impossible to feel a sustainable degree of comfort in those parts of our life if we become addictively led by ambition.

It is not far-fetched to believe that we can be "highly motivated" in our business of lawyering without deferring enjoyment of all the wonderful things we now have…without putting off the enjoyment of our possessions until we have bigger and better possessions.

We should be able to "overachieve" without needing peers, friends, and family to pay homage to our achievements.

It is not stretching the imagination to believe that we can be "masters" in our profession and still covet the intrinsic value of the many parts of life that do not pay financial dividends. For example, we can recognize that there is a value in learning new things, growing, developing new friendships, even though we can't assess that value by a monetary standard.

We should be able to be the "senior partners" of America's biggest law firms and still have a well-formulated, people-friendly vision of how much is enough for ourselves and people who are counting on us.

We should be able to be multimillion-dollar lawyers, the Best Lawyers in America, and avoid the tendency to regard family, friends, partners, and peers as a means to an end, as pawns that are there merely to move us closer to the king's square.

As our competitive edge kicks in day after day, we should be able to minimize the "me versus them" attitude that so often dehumanizes our interaction with so many people in our lives.

We cannot integrate all the worst qualities, the self-indulgent ambition into our lives as lawyers and still find any sustainable level of joy and satisfaction inside or outside our office.

The most bitter pill to swallow about what Ken Keyes and so many of his predecessors had to say is that our quality of life, our happiness, cannot be found in the power, the security, the possessions, the money, the big homes, the big cars, the airplanes or boats, the vacation homes, professional recognition, honors and accolades that we have spent our career in search of.

For most of us, it is tough to stomach the very worst of what Keyes had to say, that is, that a better quality of life is not necessarily synonymous with more money and more power. That is a tough theory for most of us to buy into because it requires us to think outside the box that we have been operating in most of our lives.

Most of us have spent much of our careers believing that once we own enough of this world, we can finally be free to do what we want and be our best selves. Ideas such as fewer clients, less money, don't fit the paradigm that we believe will bring us joy or satisfaction.

The distilled wisdom of Keyes and the philosophers that he borrowed from came down to this: *Nothing in this world should be clung to.*

In 1890, Jerome K. Jerome wrote a short satirical book titled *Three Men in a Boat.* It is a comedy about three friends who plan a week-long boat trip down the Thames River. Early in the story, Jerome has the opportunity to put down on paper his observations about possessions and power. As the three companions are loading up their boat for their week-long trip, they must decide what they need and what they want loaded into their small boat. The dialogue goes like this:

"You know, we are on the wrong track altogether. We must not think of the things we could do with, but only of the things we can't do without…"

I call that downright wisdom, not merely as regards the present case, but with reference to our trip up the river of life generally. How many people, on that voyage, load up the boat till it is in danger of swamping with a store of foolish things which they think essential to the pleasure and comfort of the trip, but which are really only useless lumber.

How they pile the poor little craft mast-high with fine clothes and big houses;…expensive entertainments that nobody enjoys, with formalities and fashions, with pretense and ostentation, and with—oh, heaviest, maddest lumber of all!—the dread of what will my

neighbor think, with luxuries that only cloy,
with pleasures that bore, with empty show that,
like the criminal's iron crown of yore, makes to
bleed and swoon the aching head that wears it!

It is lumber, man—all lumber! Throw it
overboard! It makes the boat so heavy to pull,
you nearly faint at the oars. It makes it so
cumbersome and dangerous to manage, you
never know a moment's freedom from anxiety
and care, never gain a moment's rest for
dreamy laziness....

Throw the lumber over, man! Let your boat
of life be light, packed with only what you
need—a homely home and simple pleasures,
one or two friends, worth the name, someone to
love and someone to love you, a cat, a dog, and
a pipe or two, enough to eat and enough to
wear, and a little more than enough to drink;
for thirst is a dangerous thing.

Jerome was exploring the possibility that more may
not be better long before the marketing masters on

Madison Avenue had completely unlocked virtually all doors leading to every inharmonious aspect of our ego.

Critics of Madison Avenue who have long studied the tricks of the marketing trade have developed a pretty good understanding of how modern marketers pander to most of our worst personality qualities. Authors such as John Berger and Andrew Bard Schmookler have identified the marketers' rules of engagement:

- Good marketing focuses on creating images about what we want in our immediate future. It avoids calling attention to what we now have. If we now possess Item "A," truly great marketing will cause us to defer being happy until we possess Item "B."

- Insightful marketing will force us to in some way transform our lives from the way they are now to what the marketers tell us is a more materially desirable form.

- Good marketing seeks to make us envious of other people who have these things we should want for ourselves.

- Really great marketing should successfully make the potential buyer dissatisfied with his life.
- Successful marketing will never be all that it can be unless it creates a sustainable level of anxiety for its intended audience.
- The masters of marketing understand the importance of creating a sense of scarcity in the face of abundance.
- Really sly marketing convinces the targets that if they own Item "A," they will be on their way to having *more* than their neighbor.

Throughout all of Jerome's writing career, he wrestled with understanding the destructive nature of man's unhealthy ambition. He obviously believed that the best cure for self-centered ambition began with our recognition that it causes us unhappiness. Jerome saw it this way:

It seems to be the rule of this world. Each person has what he doesn't want, and other people have what he does want.

Throwing most of our lumber overboard positively would bring more joy into our law offices and our homes. Actually getting to the place where we do it, on the other hand, sounds too much like philosophical psychobabble. We simply cannot get our mind around the concept of how being satisfied with a little less actually will improve the quality of our lives.

The truth is that the odds are against us. It is difficult to reject the wisdom of Madison Avenue when it keeps telling us that we can, and in fact, deserve to die with bigger, better, and more toys than the other guy.

The admen have perfected the art of enticing us to live well beyond our means. Madison Avenue has a great day when it produces a 30-second television spot that convinces viewers that this is acceptable. Almost 90 percent of the lawyers who responded to the questionnaire said that they believe that spending beyond their financial ability rose to the level of being destructive in the lives of some lawyers.

There are dozens of dimensions to the ways that living beyond our means can do damage to our lives. But the most obvious is that we tend to mortgage our shot at living a life with balance. We maneuver ourselves into situations where we are unable to say no to more work because our financial obligations constantly need servicing. As a result, that day when we can at last live a more relaxed, maybe even a more balanced life becomes more a pipe dream than a reality.

Buying the Image

Several years ago, I was walking through a clothing store on Fifth Avenue in New York City. It was one of the many trendy stores that occupy space on that street. It was one of those stores where it is uncool for the salespeople, who are typically dressed in black from head to toe, to pay much attention to the customers. One of those places where a kind smile from a salesclerk would be considered a fashion faux pas.

At a counter situated near the entrance to the store was a display advertising a perfume called "Egoiste." I could not bring myself to walk out of the store without striking up a conversation with the very hip-looking salesclerk standing behind that display counter.

The conversation went something like this:

"Why do you suppose they named this perfume 'Egoiste'?"

Careful not to smile and looking somewhat annoyed that I had asked her to interact with someone far less hip than herself, she replied, "Egoiste is a state of mind."

I immediately recognized that some soap peddler on Madison Avenue, some marketing think tank, had conducted a buyers' focus group and had decided that they would sell this perfume as a "state of mind." And now I stood face-to-face with part of a marketing machine who was there to reiterate that mindless theme.

So I asked, "What do you mean 'Egoiste is a state of mind'? Aren't we talking about a perfume here?"

I could have sworn I saw a sneer as she glanced over my head, focused her eyes on the wall behind me, and almost like an automaton, explained to me that Egoiste accentuates your center of power, your sense of importance. Center of power, sense of importance?

I am convinced that she was genuinely shocked when I began laughing out loud. Granted, such a reaction was inconsiderate, but in my defense, it also was not calculated. I really could not believe what I was hearing. In a second, I regained my composure. It was not right of me to openly offend her. She was, after all, only spinning a product—an image—a state of mind.

But I had to hear more. So I did what most lawyers would do. I asked, "What do you mean?" I figured these perfume peddlers had certainly armed her with more talking points.

And they had.

She went on to explain that the scent one wears influences one's "self image."

I am not certain whether it was her intent to punish me for laughing at her sales theme, for not taking her seriously, but at that moment she took on the look of someone with a mission. She threw at me the words "style," "important," "in charge," "image," "attitude," "status," and "envy," all woven together like a run-on sentence and all delivered in a matter of 30 seconds.

So I did what I was supposed to do: I bought a bottle. Even though I was not certain whether I was supposed to drink it or splash it all over my body, I recognized that it would have been foolish to pass up the opportunity to buy such an incredible product.

As I strolled back to my hotel room that day, I felt annoyed that the spin doctors on Madison Avenue had believed that they had figured me out, that they believed that they knew what drove me to achieve, to excel—and that now they had successfully put it in a bottle. They had bottled images, mental pictures, and labeled it, 'Egoiste.'

The marketing industry takes advantage of our addiction to having "more than enough." In fact, there are publications with names such as *Target Marketing* that devote a great deal of their time and resources to capitalizing on our handicaps. They view our loss as their gain. It is their business to know the qualities of our neighborhood, what we drive, our annual household income, what we buy, why we buy, and when we buy.

Target Marketing ran an article in 1998 that offers some insight into the science of marketing to lawyers. It described us as among the "country's most affluent consumers, who are time-crunched, high-income, and well educated." We are, according to *Target Marketing,* "good prospects for business apparel, financial services, insurance, travel, sports equipment," and, most importantly, "all manner of luxury products and time-saving services."

Target Marketing knew that "readers of the *American Bar Association Journal* are nearly twice as likely as readers of *Fortune* or *Business Week* to have annual household incomes higher than $200,000."

We are professionals who "must spend heavily on work wardrobes," making us "good candidates for business apparel catalogues such as *Talbots* and *Brooks Brothers*. In addition, [we] tend to be heavy travelers. Almost half of the readers of the *American Bar Association Journal* buy five or more domestic round-trip flights per year."

Target Marketing also pointed out that we are great candidates for timesaving services such as professional child care because we are working hard to provide more for our children. Furthermore, we are great candidates for hiring people to clean our bigger homes while we work to buy even bigger homes, tend to our bigger yards and gardens, clean and maintain our cars, boats, airplanes, etc.

According to the questionnaire responses below, lawyers are at least considering the impact Madison Avenue has on their lives:

Images that are sold to me by the media (e.g., magazines, TV, movies) have the following effect on my lifestyle:

I have never considered the possible impact they have on me.
Yes 24% No 76%

They push me toward greater achievement.
Yes 30% No 70%

I always recognize that they are illusory.
Yes 59% No 41%

I feel those images push me toward being more materialistic than I would prefer.
Yes 46% No 54%

I regard "trendy" people as being weak and impressionable.
Yes 60% No 40%

Although we may not see ourselves as such, marketers believe we *are* a bit "trendy" in our endless pursuit of those things that are going to make us feel more secure, more powerful—those things that will make us the object of someone else's envy. Their demographics tell them that as a group, we are always willing to load our boats down with a little more lumber. Like it or not, the marketers know that lawyers have trouble ignoring the trendiest of trendy merchandising groups, such as The Sharper Image.

For every 100,000 savvy marketers intent on pushing the envelope of America's consumerism, there are unfortunately only one or two contemporary thinkers explaining how and why our need for more has become an unhealthy addiction. Andrew Bard Schmookler is one of the greatest of those thinkers. He views the situation this way:

> My interpretation is that what people are
> seeking in wealth is not the wealth itself, but
> other things. One of these…is status: people
> feel that having greater wealth than those

around them gives them greater importance and value in other people's eyes. This means that having a little, around those who have even less, may give one more happiness than having a lot around people who have more.

Chapter Five
Thankfulness

O N A HOT SUMMER DAY, *two friends walking in the noonday sun decided that they would sit under a very old* tree to cool off in the shade that the huge limbs of the tree had created.

While they were taking advantage of the tree's shade, they became critical of the old tree. One of them pointed out that the tree was unable to bear any useful fruit. The other observed that when the leaves fell from the old tree, they made a mess on the grass and on the road.

The old tree made an observation as well. The tree observed that even as these two travelers were being cooled by the shade that the tree had to offer, they could not find it in their hearts to be thankful.

In 1955, Van Arsdale France was the person responsible for creating an "attitude manual" for Disneyland employees. The manual was an ambitious undertaking designed with the goal of helping Disney employees from top management down to project a cheerful optimism in their interaction with Disney customers.

It was France's hope that this cheerful optimism would consistently be made a part of the way Disney employees dealt with people, whether they were selling tickets for admission to the park or closing deals in multibillion-dollar real estate acquisitions.

France himself not only projected optimism in his role as a Disney employee, but from every indicator he actually was immensely satisfied and content with his life both in and out of his job. France's positive outlook on life was so consistently upbeat that co-workers at every level referred to him as Disneyland's living, breathing Jiminy Cricket.

His critics could easily argue that it is easy enough to remain upbeat when a major part of your job description involves overseeing the conduct of Dopey, Bashful, Happy, and a whole host of other fairytale and cartoon characters. Those critics would, however, need to be just a tad bit intellectually dishonest to justify such an argument. Because the truth of the matter is that France dealt every day with pressures, stresses, and chaos that would scare the hell out of most of America's busiest lawyers. France, after all, was in charge of helping to improve the attitude of tens of thousands of employees day to day during his career with one of the largest entertainment corporations in the world.

France wrote a book, *Window on Main Street,* that chronicles his many years as chief of attitude control for the entire Disney organization. It is apparent that he believed that the most basic building block for a sustainable, peaceful, optimistic, and upbeat attitude for day-to-day living was thankfulness—gratitude for what is right about our lives. He recognized that there was a direct relationship between our capacity for thankfulness and our ability to sustain our sense of peacefulness, contentment, and optimism day to day.

France's book reads like a celebration of his blessings. It is a list of his gratitudes. One almost gets the impression that he chronicled all that was pleasant, gratifying, and rewarding about his day-to-day life so that he could remind himself of things for which he wanted to remain thankful. Here is a short excerpt from *Window on Main Street:*

I'm writing this from my office/trailer in Disneyland's Circle D Ranch. This is where our "cast" of horses is housed, trained and pampered. To get here, I usually walk from the Administration Building, down Main Street, across the moat and through Fantasyland, and then through a "For Cast Members Only" gate to Backstage. Frequently I'll pause to watch the swans in the moat, and as I pass through the Sleeping Beauty Castle Entrance I take time to listen to "When You Wish Upon a Star," which has been playing since we opened.

My favorite time is early in the morning before the park opens, when the guests, God bless 'em, have not arrived to distract me. I can take the time to look around and enjoy the many creative architectural wonders which can be found in this wondrous place.…

And the trees!…These are trees we saved from death by freeway construction back in 1955. Like me, they weren't young when they were relocated here, and each one has a distinct personality, and they may be as old as I am. I feel like saluting them with "Hi! Old Timer."

The early morning is also a great time to chat with my friends who are working on final Park cleanup or preparing to open our shops for the rush of guests who will soon arrive.

We Will Feel No Thankfulness Before Its Time

When you read a passage such as the France quote above, your first thought may be that here is a person who is not confronted by the same caliber of struggles, stresses, demands, chaos, or responsibilities that face a typical lawyer. In fact, you might conclude that we can only be thankful for things such as swans in a moat, an early-morning chat with a friend, or the grandeur of an old tree when we are at a special time in our lives. Perhaps that special time is when we get to the place where we are no longer fighting the ever-present wolves at our door, or perhaps that time will occur after we have built America's biggest law firm or when we get our children through college.

The truth is, it makes us feel better to rationalize that the natural order of life is such that we are not supposed to take time to be grateful for large or small blessings before the time when we are through with our struggling...or before the time when we have brought permanent order to all the chaos in our lives.

France believed differently. He recognized that we improve the quality of our lives in all respects when we are thankful for what we have now or for who we are today. Most of us, on the other hand, are always working toward a time or waiting for a time when we will be thankful for what we have or who we are, as if our capacity for thankfulness would improve over time like some fine vintage wine.

But the bad news is that our capacity to be thankful does not mystically improve by itself over time. In fact, our capacity to be grateful is likely to become atrophied after too many years of disuse.

That curmudgeonly old judge we are forced to practice in front of or that miserable old law partner that we have to pass in the halls of our office every day worked decades to arrive at their level of thanklessness. While they were cultivating their ability to remain ungrateful for their successes, blessings, and overall good fortune, Van Arsdale France in his 87 years of life was developing his special technique for remaining thankful.

When it comes to thinking about ways to help people improve their quality of life, you will always find an abundance of great thinkers. The same is true of the art of being thankful. Van Arsdale France was not the first thinker to try to engineer a technique for remaining thankful: sometime around 60 B.C., for example, Cicero analyzed the issue this way; "Gratitude is not only the greatest of virtues, but the parent of all others."

So how do we develop a healthy capacity for gratitude? Answers to such questions often depend on whom you talk to, but that is not the case with this question. There seems to be some uniformity in the recommended way to get there.

To Be Thankful, Avoid Comparisons

Herb Sadler, the author of *Today Is the Only Day,* has formulated a technique for transforming our mindset from one of ingratitude for almost everything to thankfulness for those blessings that are barely noticeable to us most of the time.

Sadler is of the opinion that the transformation begins with a commitment not to compare ourselves to others. It is unlikely that we can ever fully appreciate who we are or what is good about our life if our focus is too fixed on someone who obviously has more. When we live in an endless state of comparison, chances are we are more conscious of the other person's blessings than of our own. We convince ourselves that the lawyer down the street is living a life that has more quality, excitement, glamour, or success than ours because he has more things. Or maybe his life is more complete and overall better because he appears to have a better marriage or fewer problems with his children.

Statistically, that person we are comparing ourselves to is also comparing himself to someone else up the street. When we compare our blessings to the blessings we perceive that others have, we believe the process aids us in arriving at our level of self-worth. We after all need to compare ourselves to others to determine how we are *progressing* in this competitive world of lawyering…don't we? Most of the time, it is easier to count and be desirous of his blessings than to even acknowledge, much less be grateful for, our own.

Living with the "H" Word

There is usually a common theme in books that tell us that we will improve the quality of our lives, that we will be more optimistic, more content and peaceful day to day, when we learn the art of thankfulness. That common theme is that we must incorporate a little *humility* into our personality profile.

This thought is attributed to Henry Ward Beecher, a nineteenth-century social reform advocate: "A proud man is seldom a grateful man, for he never thinks he gets as much as he deserves."

The next time you go to a birthday party for a child between the ages of two and six, you can get a clearer picture of what Beecher meant. Chances are you will see the child (not our own, of course) tearing her way through the gaudy wrapping paper of one present after another as fast as her small hands can move. You will notice that she barely pauses long enough between gifts to actually acknowledge—or realize—what she has been given. That child is only receiving what she believes she deserves. It is her birthday, after all. Those presents, according to her underdeveloped world view, are hers as a matter of right. In fact, regardless of the number of presents she receives, there is a very high probability that she will believe she is entitled to even more.

That type of conduct is understandable when we are analyzing the developing ego of a four-year-old. Humble gratitude is rarely to be expected. But shouldn't we be expecting more of ourselves between the ages of 24 and 74?

One impediment to overcoming our tendency to consistently think like the four-year-old at her birthday party is that most of us have convinced ourselves that the type of humility contemplated by Beecher is more appropriately reserved for hopeless underachievers. After all, how can we be humble when we have accomplished so much?

The Fear of Being Thankful

When Copernicus suggested to the world that the earth was not the center of our solar system, his contemporaries asked him to reconsider his theory or face the wrath of the Catholic church. Up to the time that Copernicus made such a suggestion, the world's leadership had bought into Aristotle's theory that the universe was finite and that that finite cosmos had the earth at the center, with man in control of that earth.

Copernicus and later Galileo were the proponents of a theory that caused fear in the minds of thinkers and philosophers who felt comfortable with the notion that man was the master of his universe. The type of heresy suggested by Copernicus could only lead man to conclude that he is not in control of all of the events that improve or detract from his quality of life.

Since the time Copernicus told us the truth about the cosmos, not much has changed about man's desire to believe that he is in control of most earthly events. It puts us at ease to convince ourselves that we control our lives almost entirely by our hard work, limitless imagination, and vast intellect. Most of us believe that we have accomplished great things in our lives almost entirely because we have more talent, drive, and savvy than our neighbor.

When we allow ourselves to say that we deserve to be who we are and where we are solely because of our unique efforts, we eliminate all that hocus pocus about good fortune, grace, and blessings having any significant impact on our lives. Likewise, when we too often allow ourselves to show gratitude and thankfulness for all the aspects of our lives that are pleasing or rewarding, we are in a sense acknowledging that we have been given something that we have not earned by our own efforts.

That makes many of us uneasy because if we acknowledge that we have gained something that we do not entirely deserve, that something has been given to us over which we had no control, then we must also acknowledge that it can be taken away in the same fashion. It is more comforting to believe that everything we have, whether it is influence, affluence, prestige, security, even good health, we have because we work hard enough and smart enough to deserve it.

We feel more in control when we see a direct relationship between our efforts and our rewards. In our mind, it is our efforts and talent alone that will put us and keep us where we are in the world.

For example, if each day we engage in the "mystical" or "mysterious" routine of somehow acknowledging that we are thankful for our health, aren't we also acknowledging that we may not have complete control over that aspect of our lives? Isn't it true that implicit in that acknowledgment of thankfulness is also the acknowledgment that no matter how hard we exercise, no matter how closely we watch our diet, our health may still be at risk without good fortune on our side?

For most of us, there is a less disturbing analysis. It is to avoid the burden of routinely being thankful and rely exclusively on ourselves by increasing reps at the gym and obsessing about what we eat or drink. That way we alone are in control and more importantly there is less need to be fearful that our good health will ever be lost because by our very own effort and will, we will not permit it to be so.

Taking Inventory

Mythology, philosophy, and almost every brand of religion have always had a few mean edges mixed in with any advice that they delivered about better-quality living.

One of those mean edges is that we are always at risk of forever losing the things that we value. In fact, even the things we love and cherish are constantly in peril from forces way beyond our control.

Mythology and all disciplines of religion have left us an almost endless array of ugly short stories and sagas about men and women who abruptly lost what they cherished and, at the same time, took for granted.

Mythical gods and goddesses played a role in Jason's losing valued possessions, best friends, and even his family while he struggled to grasp a golden fleece always just beyond his reach. All the while, he never showed a capacity for appreciating the fact that his Argonaut friends were fearlessly loyal and that he

171

was loved, missed, and appreciated back home whether he returned with a fleece or not. During Jason's 20-year voyage, he battled 100-foot bronze giants and seven-headed snake monsters, not to mention an army of skeletons, to acquire that one special thing for which he could possibly be thankful.

One sobering theme to the story is that we never have permanent ownership of our good fortune. Jason was continually being shown that virtually all of his blessings and good fortune vanished almost as quickly as they appeared. The best things in his life at any given time were only transitory, and if today he missed the opportunity to be thankful and appreciative, he might never get the chance because those things could suddenly be taken from him.

Mankind's great religions have also devoted a huge amount of written word to trying to cajole us into taking constant inventory of what is pleasing about our lives today because those pleasing things may be gone tomorrow. The teaching examples used to deliver the message may differ among the various religions, but the message is the same: Take inventory of what you have, and be thankful for what you have while you can.

A Tibetan Buddhist monk might illustrate his point by spending months creating an intricately detailed picture with fine colored sand which he will then completely obliterate with the brush of his hands in less than a matter of seconds. Meticulously working on his sand mandala may have brought him joy every day of the year while it was being created. He may have found joy each day in knowing that he had the talent, imagination, and physical ability to create such a phenomenal work of art. But his religious teachings direct him to be reminded of that transitory joy during the seconds it takes him to destroy his own creation.

The Old Testament has a much meaner edge in the way it makes its point about the need to take inventory and be thankful for what we have today because we may not have it tomorrow. Job is almost the perfect poster boy for that message in the Old Testament. In that story, a completely decent, blameless man suffers the loss of virtually everything he owns and cherishes as his loyalty to his God is tested.

A tornado kills all of his children, roving gangs steal his cattle and kill his loyal servants, lightning strikes and burns up his sheep and his herdsmen, and he is plagued with horrible disease. The happy ending to the story is that Job remains constant in his faith throughout all these tests, and, as a result, his blessings are restored. There are dozens of lessons that can be lifted from the Job story, but one of those lessons is certainly that the impermanence of all our blessings is a reality that mankind lives with everyday.

Taking Away the Big Bone

There is a negotiating technique that many of us have seen used from time to time in our law practice. It is called "the takeaway." It is usually used at a time when both sides are reasonably close to negotiating a resolution to a dispute. Both sides are at a point where they could be happy with the terms of the proposed settlement, but one side wants more. Possibly that one side wants to overreach and maybe get a little greedy with its demands. The experienced negotiator will often attempt to bring that overreaching party back to reality with the announcement that all offers are withdrawn.

All of a sudden that lawyer who was intent on over-reaching begins to realize that this perfectly good deal has been taken away. His thinking shifts from how he can get more to how he can get back what he already had.

There is nothing like the takeaway to make someone take inventory of what is good and pleasing about what he had. What he took for granted and could barely appreciate yesterday suddenly begins to look like something that he cannot live without today. It is at that time when he fears that he has lost what he once had that he very seriously begins to take inventory of how his life might be affected by that loss.

There is a quality that is characteristic of many ambitious people. It is a quality that causes the newness of the cars they drive or the homes they build to wear off faster than it might with their less ambitious neighbor. This quality too often causes them to take the happiness that they experience with their spouse and children for granted. They seldom even acknowledge that they have a quality of life that is most likely better than that of 90 percent of the rest of the world. The only time they might even take notice of their good health is when they hear about the death or crippling illness of some friend or acquaintance that they consider similarly situated in the world.

Aesop described the risk of not being thankful for what we already have this way:

A dog found one of the biggest bones he had ever found in his many years of looking for bones. He was hurrying home with this perfect bone when he came to a bridge that crossed a small lake. As the dog was crossing the lake, he noticed, down in the water, the image of a dog with a bone that looked even bigger than his. He didn't realize that what he was looking at was actually his reflection in the calm water.

Instead of being grateful for the bone that he had, he dropped his bone and sprang after the dog with the better, more pleasing-looking bone. When he jumped into the water after that better bone, he realized that there was not another dog—there was not a bigger, better bone. As he struggled to swim to the shore of that lake, he also realized that he had lost the biggest and best bone that he had ever found in his many years of looking for bones.

Chapter Six
Joy

AN ASS HEARD SEVERAL GRASSHOPPERS *chirping a cheerful song in a field where he was grazing. The noise they were making was so filled with joy that the ass was curious about what caused them to have such a jovial spirit.*

The ass wanted to lift his spirit as high as the spirit of those grasshoppers, so he asked the grasshoppers what allowed them to sing so beautifully. He asked them if they ate some special, mysterious food or if they had discovered some rare nectar that was unknown to other creatures.

The grasshoppers jokingly told the poor dumb ass that yes, they had made a spectacular discovery. They told him that it was the dew off the grass that lifted their spirit and allowed them to sing. After that day, the ass ate nothing and would drink nothing but dew.

As you might expect, the spirit of the poor, dumb ass did not soar any higher, and he soon died.

Relaunching the Spirit

Just to the north of Athens, Greece, lies the ancient city of Delphi. The Delphians believed that their city sat exactly at the center of the earth. The leadership at Delphi, along with promoting the belief that their city was the center of the ancient world, were also proud of the mystery and reputation of their very own oracle. For centuries, on the seventh day of every month, the priestess of Apollo would prophesy for anyone who could afford her services.

The oracle made Delphi a very important place around 600 B.C. To honor Apollo (the city's patron god), the Delphic oracle, and even the citizens of Delphi, kings from all over ancient Greece would send gold, jewelry, precious stones, and artwork of all descriptions to be deposited in Delphi's treasury. This Delphic civilization was regarded as being an enlightened one. The city and its citizens were held in high esteem by the rest of the ancient world.

Aesop was asked by the king he served to go to Delphi and distribute money among its citizens. It was his king's way of paying homage. The very little history that was recorded about Aesop's journey to Delphi does not tell us much about why this journey resulted in the tragic end to Aesop's life. But we do know that Aesop was not impressed with Delphi or its citizens. His short time there did not lead him to conclude that this civilization was enlightened. We at least know that Aesop did not believe that the citizens of Delphi were worthy of his king's homage.

It is always difficult to judge the accuracy of reconstructed history, but the history that is available helps us draw a few conclusions about what went wrong for Aesop during his stay in Delphi.

Aesop's philosophy spoke about the wisdom of simpler living. His philosophy placed a high value on serving and giving to others. He believed in the wisdom of honesty about our importance in the world. Moderation in all things was an underlying theme to Aesop's formula for maintaining a joyful spirit. But there was nothing simple, moderate, charitable, or humble about the civilization that Aesop encountered. Forty-foot marble statues honoring the god Apollo and his friends lined the streets and walkways all around the city. The Delphians coveted their temples and monuments. In their treasuries, they hoarded more ivory, gold, silver, and bronze artwork than could be found in almost any part of that ancient world.

Aesop's formula for finding and maintaining joy in his life was greatly at odds with the beliefs of the average citizen of Delphi. He concluded that those people of Delphi were not worthy of his master's tribute of gold, and he therefore refused to give that gold to them.

The philosophy that Aesop preached in Delphi so outraged the citizens that a mob took him prisoner, beat him nearly to death, then threw his body over a sheer rock cliff.

We can only speculate about whether it was his message or his failure to deliver his master's money that caused the mob to kill Aesop that day.

G. K. Chesterton was a nineteenth-century author and journalist who may be best known for his essays and short stories examining the advantages of moderate living.

Chesterton wrote an introduction to an edition of Aesop's Fables. In that introduction, he provides some insight into what kind of message could be found in the philosophy of Aesop. He writes;

> The firm foundations of common sense, the shrewd shots at uncommon sense that characterize all the fables, belong not to Aesop, but to humanity in the earliest human history. Whatever is authentic is universal.

Chesterton goes on to explain that these universally authentic truths were merely restated by Aesop. Aesop was not responsible for any original thought when he illustrated these truths by showing how the good or bad deeds, the kindness or cruelty, the arrogance or humility, the character or lack of it altered the lives of the animals and people in his stories. Chesterton's point, of course, is that some truths don't ever change; we just forget that they exist, or perhaps we never learned them, or maybe it is just that we fail to believe in them. He points out that it is those kinds of truths that mankind has the hardest time accepting.

The literature of great thinkers such as Homer, King David, King Solomon, and others was available to Aesop when he created his animal fables. That literature stated and restated most of the universal truths and the commonsense wisdom that surface in Aesop's fables.

One of those truths is that there is a relationship between the quality of our lives and the quality of our spirit. In fact, if you analyze the advice of mankind's greatest sages, you would have to conclude that our quality of life is more dependent on a healthy, joyful spirit than on our possessions and relative position of power and influence in the world.

But those sages also tell us that characters like the ass in Aesop's fable will forever complicate the process of developing a joyful spirit. They tell us that characters like the ass will continually be led to all the wrong places in their effort to lift their spirit.

Aesop left us dozens of fables that urge us to reject the advice of characters like the grasshopper who would send us on an endless, fruitless quest for some magical nectar that would allow us to maintain a joyful spirit. Aesop left us stories that lead us to conclude that a healthy spirit is not necessarily dependent on acquiring all of the most attractive "things" our popular culture has to offer.

The lesson Aesop leaves us in his fable about the ass and the grasshopper would not have been easily accepted or believed by the citizens of Delphi. Likewise, Aesop's lesson about a joyful spirit not being dependent on anything we can possess in this world does not have the ring of an authentic truth to most of us practicing law today.

Believing Our Instincts

Jacob Nedelman, the author of *Money and Meaning of Life*, tells us that we program ourselves to look for joy in all the wrong places. Nedelman believes that most of us have wiser, more enlightened "old souls" that we lose touch with as we scramble to get more and achieve more. He says that we are quick to buy into what almost everyone else tells us will bring us a joyful spirit, but we hardly ever trust our own instincts about cultivating joy.

For example, a young lawyer should know instinctively that being employed at a law firm that requires her to work

80 hours a week to make her billable-hour requirements will not provide much lift to the spirit. However, when she is told enough times by enough people that to do so is normal, acceptable, even honorable, she is willing, in fact even anxious, to give her life away in 80-hour increments. Just like the ass, she becomes a true believer in what she has been told, and she ignores what her instincts must surely be telling her.

Has she actually found joy in a process that inevitably dulls not only the spirit but also the character and intellect, or has merely she bought into the myth that the process will infuse joy into her spirit sometime in the future? Does she imagine that if she can just ignore her instincts and believe what the rest of the lawyering world is telling her, then a healthy, uplifted spirit is just a few years away?

I am regularly asked by lawyer organizations to give speeches about many of the topics covered in this book. Often when I give those speeches, I find that senior partners in both large corporate defense firms and moderate-to-large claimant firms loath any discussion of the threat of overworking the mind and the body to the point that the spirit suffers. They, after all, have a vested financial interest in minimizing the importance of such discussions. The reaction of these senior partners and managing partners does not strike me as being odd in any way—short sighted, but not odd. On the other hand, the interesting reaction to my message by the young associate who is willing to fritter his life away as a billable-hour slave does sometimes strike me as odd.

Job dissatisfaction among young lawyers in large-to-medium-sized firms is higher than it has ever been. But the young lawyers continue to fill those "bill mill" positions because of the unspoken promise that has been developed and promoted within the lawyer culture for so many decades. That promise is: "Defer your joy today, and you will experience greater joy in the future." The suggestion is that we should move between two extremes: 20 years of living a life that is torturous to a healthy spirit in exchange for 10 more years of joyful living. There are a few problems with that unspoken promise, the least of which is that real life rarely lives up to that promise. There are some empirical data that prove it is not true, and there are some logical reasons that help us understand why it will never be true.

Those reasons begin with the fact that we are creatures of habit. Regardless of how much intellectual acumen we believe we have, our good sense and our intellect play second and third fiddle to our habits. For example, if you were to follow the life and 30-year career of one or two of those senior partners who chose to habitually sacrifice all now in order to be eternally joyful sometime in the future, you will notice that that healthy spirit still probably has not broken through the surface.

Chances are it never will break through because the lawyer's habits for 30 years did not include developing a joyful spirit. He has become a product of the environment that was probably initially structured not by him, but by someone else 30 years ago—but an environment that he nonetheless voluntarily chose to be a part of for 30 years. The trap is often the same for lawyers whether they work in a billable-hour shop or in a contingency fee operation.

I have worked for the same law firm for 18 years. It is a firm that for 50 years exclusively handled claimants' cases for a contingency fee. We have had as many as 40 lawyers working in our firm. And in the Southeast, we probably are one of the largest claimants' firms around. I have always tried to analyze the people and the workings of our law firm as a microcosm of the legal profession. When I obtain data of any kind about lawyers, I try to compare those data with what I can readily observe in my own backyard.

In the process of writing three books about lawyers and the profession of lawyering, I have observed all the positives and all the negatives that I have ever written about through the doors of the office that I have occupied at this firm. Through those office doors, looking both out and in, I have learned quite a lot about all the good parts and the bad parts of lawyering. I have learned something about this topic of living and lawyering with a healthy, joyful spirit.

Building from the Inside Out

I have learned that in order to maintain a healthy spirit in the practice of law, you must build your practice from the inside out. You must begin the process by deciding what kind of life you want and then build your practice around that life. It is the type of decision that so dramatically affects your life and the lives of all your family members that you cannot allow someone else to make that decision for you. You cannot buy into legends or popular myths about what type of lawyering life will bring you happiness. You must do what you have been trained to do: you must ask tough questions, kick over a few rotted logs, and be willing to reject what everyone around you has so willingly accepted.

In order to build your practice from the inside out, you cannot be willing to be anyone's "boy." If you instinctively recognize that something doesn't fit, then don't force it. Old myths and legends will not provide you with the reliable advice you will get from the instinct you have lived with all your life.

Aesop had a theory that when we don't pay attention to what our instincts tell us, then we begin making personal compromises to our own detriment. Here is how Aesop delivered that warning:

A very wealthy man moved into a house that was located next door to a leather tanner. The man at first recognized that the tanning process created a nauseatingly unpleasant odor, and so he complained and asked the tanner to move his business somewhere else. In fact, the wealthy and influential man put pressure on the tanner several times, demanding that he move his tanning business immediately. The clever tanner, however, delayed his move time and again, always promising either that the smell would soon go away or that he would move. As time passed, the wealthy man became used to the putrid smell that was created at the tannery, and, just as the tanner had expected, the wealthy man accepted the smell as normal and quit complaining.

Lawyers by the tens of thousands every day compromise their instincts the same way that the wealthy man chose to compromise his. Just like the wealthy man in the fable, we allow ourselves to accept what should be unacceptable. We are quick to trade our sense of joy for a bag full of cash.

At our firm, I have seen older partners who have acquired fortunes greater than those of 95 percent of the lawyers in this country, but still a joyful spirit escapes them. On the other hand, I have for 18 years observed the lives of older partners in my firm who have overcome those odd problems that often accompany real fortune and real fame, and they have held onto their sense of joy. Their sense of joy about their life as a lawyer has actually matured.

I have discovered a powerful difference between those two classes of lawyers. The consistent, predictable, unshakable difference is that the joyless lawyer somewhere along the line developed his life around a type of practice that he did not love. The other group, on the other hand, first figured out what type of life they wanted to live and then doggedly built the type of practice they enjoyed around the type of lifestyle that they wanted for themselves. It is easy to be joyless, but developing sustainable joy takes some commitment and hard work.

Building your practice from the inside out requires you to make some unequivocal choices. What types of cases do you really want to handle? How answerable will you allow yourself to be to an employer or law partners who want to tell you how to work or when to work or how fast you can progress in your skill as a lawyer? How dependent on some other person do you want to be when it comes to determining your level of income? How much time do *you* want to spend working each week, and how much time you want to spend with your family? In what type of environment do you want to practice law—big city or small town? How committed are you to creating rewarding opportunity for yourself rather than being satisfied with whatever kind of opportunity presents itself? These are the types of very preliminary questions that you have to consider in order to build your practice from the inside out. It requires that you listen to what your instincts can tell you rather than rely on what lawyer culture myths have to say about what you should do.

In the last several decades, that lawyer culture myth has led too many lawyers to believe that the lawyer who acquires the most of everything will know sustainable joy. We have had more than our share of "Exhibit 'A's" around our law firm that prove there is hardly any truth to that myth. It is, however, a powerful myth to overcome.

Because of the strength of that myth, it is not only managing partners of large law firms that often glare at me with disdain when I discuss the topic of building a law practice from the inside out. It is very often the youngest of the associates who work for those senior partners. In fact, I have had very young lawyers walk out during my speech when I get to the part where I tell them that they can find greater joy as a lawyer by building a practice centered in a lifestyle that pleases them today—a practice that passes their smell test *today*. They most of the time do not want to hear that that lifestyle that is supposed to bring them so much joy 20 years from now rarely comes to pass. They will not accept the idea that if they do not find a way to build a practice that will bring them joy today, then it is unlikely that things will change much 20 years from now. They often are even less able to get their arms around the idea that all of their many years of deferring their joy for their job and their joy for life will not be justified by the wealth and prestige that sticks to them along the way. The level of joy they are able to know today within the career they now have will likely be as good as it gets for them.

It is sometimes difficult for lawyers who have practiced for less than 10 years to even consider the need to build a practice from the inside out. It is advice that invalidates a lot of what they have been told by other, more experienced lawyers who might benefit from the young lawyers' inappropriate and unhealthy sacrifice.

For 18 years, I have listened to one of my partners grumble about how unhappy he is with the type of practice he has. His level of discontent with his practice has often had a host of negative influences on his life outside his practice. He is a talented lawyer with enough intellect, savvy, and skill to have made a good living practicing virtually any type of law he wanted. But at some point early on in his career, he concluded that the money was much too good to make an effort to please his sense of joy. Instead, he stuck with a practice he at times abhorred, all the while believing that his sense of joy might someday soar when his practice became more and more lucrative. The success of his practice has been huge, but that sense of joy still, to this day, has not developed. He was never able to believe that you can build a practice that you love—a practice that is financially successful, and, most important, a practice that allows you to feel a sense of joy about what you are doing today rather than some elusive day in the future. It is my guess that he quit believing what his senses were telling him.

When we begin believing that we can actually have some control over how well our sense of joy is able to function day to day, we then can begin to analyze a methodology for sustaining that joy. We can figure out how to fashion our lives both inside and outside our practice in a way that makes the maintenance of a joyful spirit a high priority.

It is not only our satisfaction with the size of our firm or our area of practice or the number of hours we work that has an impact on our sense of joy as a lawyer. Those things are simply a part of the total equation. We are unwilling to accept what should be reasonably apparent if we are paying attention.

Writers of self-help books are forever trying to create a kind of step-by-step methodology for capturing and perpetuating joy. In the process, they often offer suggestions that border on the ridiculous. Books with titles like *99 Ways to Find Joy* tell us that if we take hot baths at night, get regular manicures, and eat more chocolate ice cream, then surely joy will always be right within our grasp.

The appeal of these "joy books" in our culture is that they allow us to avoid making any significant decisions about long-term lifestyle changes. Instead, they suggest that the method for sustainable joy can be reduced to mostly superficial adjustments in our daily routine living. They tell us to buy desk calendars that urge us to "smile" and "be nice to ourselves." It is this type of calendar wisdom that is supposed to transform our dulled sense of joy to a perpetual jubilance.

Aesop had a notion that joyful living might require some pretty fundamental adjustments to the ways we look for joy. It is unlikely that Aesop's philosophy about joyful living could ever be reduced to the type of easy quote wisdom found in most of the joy books being sold today.

He left us with formulas for finding joy that unfortunately require some sacrifices, some elemental adjustments to the way that most of us live. He pointed out that most of us have a few personal "issues" to deal with before we can ever be joyful.

A Better Perspective on Our Self-importance

For example, Aesop tells us that most of us will need to have a better perspective about the space we occupy on a planet that is four billion years old. Aesop left us this:

The Roman god Mercury wanted to have a clear picture of how he was regarded by mankind. So he took on the form of a man and walked into a sculptor's shop. He noticed a statue of the god Jupiter and asked the shopkeeper about the price. He was told it sold for only ten drachma, and that caused Mercury to laugh at the fact that such a low value was placed on the importance of Jupiter.

Mercury then asked about the price of a statue of Juno. When the shopkeeper told him five drachma, Mercury became even more prideful and even contemptuous toward Juno because mankind valued her only half as much as Jupiter.

Finally, Mercury made the mistake of pointing to a statue of himself and asking about the selling price. The shopkeeper told him that if he would buy the other two statues he could have the Mercury statue thrown in for free.

Aesop did not end this fable with a superficial feel-good solution to the problem that Mercury had to overcome. But he did show us that Mercury's lack of perspective on his own importance probably brought him unhappiness on this occasion and would continue to bring him unhappiness on many more occasions unless he was able to pull off some pretty serious character rebuilding.

Aesop wrote at least a dozen fables that urged readers to overcome their need to feel superior to their neighbors. His fables advise us that it is difficult to be joyful when we are forever living with a skewed perspective of our importance.

I received an unusual Christmas card from a reasonably well-known, very talented, and financially successful trial lawyer. It was a "greeting" card that purported to send "warm wishes" to me for the holidays. The multiple-paneled card had pictures of this fine

lawyer standing alone in various rooms of his palatial home. One picture was a full-length body shot of him standing alone, tuxedo-clad, in front of a Steinway grand piano and what appeared to be a large antique Italian harp in his huge music room. In still another picture, he was standing alone waving at me from his beautifully decorated grand foyer. And on the back of the card, he had included a large picture of himself standing alone in front of a very expensive-looking Rolls-Royce and Porsche Cabriolet.

It was a holiday greeting card that did not really appear to be designed to send "warm wishes" to his family, friends, and acquaintances. Instead, it was a card that allowed him to validate his sense of self-importance. It was a collection of images that was designed to place a value—a net worth—on the importance of the lawyer smiling back at me in those pictures. They were the pictures of a lawyer who had made the same mistake that Mercury made when he set out to discover whether or not his sense of self-worth was consistent with how he was regarded by the world at large. The lawyer in that picture had the same problem Mercury had with his perspective of his importance.

Serving and Sharing from a Safe Distance

Aesop uses his fables to tell us something else about maintaining joy in our lives. He tells us that there is a great deal of joy to be found in the act of giving. He urges us to not be stingy or miserly in the way we share our talent and our possessions.

With his fables, he warns us that our talents and our possessions will never bring us much joy unless we use them to create happiness for others. This is one of those fables that asks us to make very difficult adjustments to our lives. It is one of those truths that become less believable to us the more successful we become.

A man who was known in his community as a miser had throughout his life hoarded large sums of gold. He had buried his huge stash of gold in his yard. The only pleasure the old man knew was to dig up and count his gold each night. One night, a thief noticed where the old man had buried his gold and easily made away with the cache while the old miser slept.

The next day the miser noticed that his gold had been stolen. It caused him such anguish that he began wailing and screaming. He was so overcome with despair that he wept like a child.

A stranger passing by the miser's yard asked him what had happened. The miser tried to explain, but the stranger did not understand why the miser would bury his gold instead of using it to buy things that he might need.

The miser answered that he would never dream of actually spending the gold on anyone or anything.

The stranger then picked up a handful of rocks and wisely told the old miser to bury the rocks. The stranger pointed out that the buried rocks would provide as much pleasure to the old man as the buried gold since the miser made no use of the gold anyway.

More than 600 years after Aesop created the fable of the miser, the universal truth that was the theme to that fable resurfaced in a parable that Jesus delivered to his followers. He told a story about a wealthy man who had given three of his slaves an equal share of money. The man then left on a trip. When he returned, he asked each of the three slaves what he had done with his gift. The first two slaves told the man that they had put the gift to use and made it productive. The third slave, on the other hand, had wrapped his money in a handkerchief and hid it so it would not be lost or taken from him. But the money *was* taken from the third slave. The man took it back and split it between the two slaves who had understood the wisdom of making the gift they possessed useful and productive.

Similar parables can be found in the Talmud, the Koran, and in the Upanishads because the lesson that surfaces in such parables is a truth that is, in the words of G. K. Chesterton, "authentic." The message has its foundation in common sense. According to Chesterton, we can dress that authentic message up any way we want, we can shake it up, mix it up, modify it with as many variables as we want, and the wisdom will still be evident.

When we fail to use our intellect, our insights and skills, our material possessions in a way that is productive for something or someone besides ourselves, then we develop qualities that are not much different from the worst qualities of the miser in Aesop's fable. As a result, the world around us suffers and our sense of joy becomes stale and dulled.

As you read this chapter about bolstering your sense of joy in your life inside and outside your law office, you probably already fall into one of several categories in the way you regard the importance of giving and serving.

1. You believe there is no connection between the level of joy in your life and giving, but you participate in such things as pro bono work and community service because of appearance requirements and because it helps further your career.

2. You have seen that there is a relationship between the two in your life, and you regularly work at better

refining your commitment to serve and give because of the joy it brings you.

3. You feel sympathy and kinship with Aesop's miser character and you regard this discussion about giving, service, and joy as whimsical nonsense.

Ken Keyes, the author of *Handbook to Higher Consciousness,* had a theory that it was exceedingly uncommon for the average person to want to graciously give to and serve others. His belief was that most of us are so intent on storing up as much as we can for some time in the future that we are usually fearful about letting go of much at all. Keyes believed that our need to feel secure not just today, but also 20 or 30 years from now, makes us worry about sharing our possessions or our energy, talent, and skills. Throughout most of our lives, according to Keyes, we are hoarding those things much like Aesop's miser. Keyes believed that arriving at the place where giving and serving leaves us joyful instead of fearful requires some pretty serious inner work. Getting to that place involves an evolution for most of us, and really being able to claim a complete victory for ourselves is improbable. Keyes would say that most of us fall into categories 1 and 3 above and that category 2 is for people who are not only caring and compassionate but also more courageous than most of us.

In the last decade, lawyers' willingness to participate in pro bono service has not changed much. Depending on which numbers you want to believe, about 25 to 30 percent of lawyers choose to participate in voluntary pro bono programs that give aid to abused children, the poor, the homeless, the handicapped, the elderly, or the environment. One survey that was conducted by the Office of Court Administration for the State of New York told us that, in that state at least, lawyers contributed a whopping $82 apiece to legal service organizations each year.

There simply is no statistical material available that we can draw upon to conclude that lawyers as a group have a charitable, giving way about them. Statistics might reasonably lead us to believe that a recognition of the relationship between joy and charitable service is lost on the majority of lawyers. There obviously are the exceptions.

A Profile of Courage

Around 1986, Robert F. Kennedy, Jr., stated in an interview that he had discovered one of those authentic truths that G. K. Chesterton says are part of the alphabet of humanity. Kennedy said in that interview that he had discovered that "It is more important to be of service than to be successful by our cultural standards." With an undergraduate degree from Harvard, a law degree from the University of Virginia, and almost unfathomable opportunity to grow into whatever he chose to be, he chose to be a servant. He and a friend, John Cronin, started one of the most effective environmental activist groups in America, called Riverkeepers. He took advocacy skills that could have brought him a staggering income as a claimants' lawyer or a corporate defense lawyer, and he lent those skills to an American environmental movement that was floundering. He took his savvy, his vision, and his leadership skills and lent them to an environmentalist community that desperately needed a jumpstart. Just about any sector of corporate America would have paid stellar salaries and bonuses in exchange for that skill and savvy.

Robert Kennedy could have buried way more than his fair share of gold in his backyard to gratify only his selfish concerns, just like Aesop's miser. He could easily have chosen to hoard his possessions, his talents—even his name—by using them in a way that would have made him wealthier, even more influential, and more successful by our skewed cultural standards. In 1985, however, he let go of the hoarder's mentality. He overcame what many of us are not courageous enough to overcome, that is, our fear that we will not *have* enough and *be* enough tomorrow if we give away too much of ourselves and our things today.

In mustering the courage to let go of his attachment to such fears, Kennedy found the kind of joy that Ken Keyes and Jacob Nedelman believed few of us would ever allow ourselves to know. Kennedy devotes almost all of his 14- and 15-hour working days to a law practice that bolsters his capacity to be joyful. It is unlikely that most of us can make such a total commitment to serving something other than ourselves, but we should be able to divide our energy and resources in a way that moves us in that direction.

Aesop said, "It is easy to be brave from a safe distance." For example, it takes less courage to commit to serving a cause when the only motivation for our service is to win our local pro bono award or move ourselves closer to some coveted professional recognition that will somehow enhance our legal career. It does not require much courage to give or serve when our goal is to get something for ourselves in the process.

On the other hand, giving a substantial amount of time or money to a soup kitchen or a hospice where we receive no professional recognition…where we make real personal sacrifices…where no one knows about those sacrifices…where our career does not benefit… where there is no pecuniary gain, requires real courage.

We are not able to make those kinds of sacrifices from a safe distance. But when we do make those types of sacrifices of ourselves and our things, we move ourselves frightfully close to real joy.

Chapter Seven
Bigger Than Life

A BULL WAS WALKING *through a marsh, startling the tiny frogs that lived there. This creature was much bigger than anything the frogs were used to seeing in their normal frog lives, and they ran away in terror.*

They related what they had seen to the bullfrog, who was the biggest frog in their frog community. The bullfrog puffed himself up and said to the other frogs, "I'll bet he was not bigger than this."

The other frogs said, "Oh, yes, he was, Mr. Bullfrog."

The prideful bullfrog, not to be outdone, puffed himself up even more until his stomach was twice its normal size. "I am certain that the creature was not bigger than this," he boasted.

But the other frogs had to break to him the troubling news that the creature was in fact much bigger. The bullfrog said, "Impossible," and then continued to puff himself up even more until he exploded.

Aesop left us with his theory that most of us do not recognize that there is often a huge cost when we attempt to be bigger than real life.

This headline appeared in the *San Francisco Chronicle* on December 9, 1995: "BELLI, 88, FILES FOR BANKRUPTCY; FABLED CAREER NEARING END, SOME FEAR."

In the story that followed, William Carlson, a staff writer, painted a disturbing picture of a legendary trial lawyer whose life had turned upside-down in the last few years of his life. This short news story in one paragraph reminds us that it was this lawyer who had acquired the title of "King of Torts." It was this lawyer who had pioneered the use of demonstrative evidence in trial. It was this lawyer who dominated the plaintiff's practice of law by once building one of the most lucrative, prestigious trial practices in America.

The other paragraphs of that story tell us about an 88-year-old trial lawyer who was embroiled in a disastrous divorce from his fifth wife. A "legendary trial lawyer" whose place in the world at that time was described as "tragic" by one of his law partners. He owed more than 120 creditors in excess of $350,000. His relationship with his former law partners had become messy to the point that he referred to them as "bums," and they described him as his "own worst enemy."

I had, of course, many times said that about people myself over this or that personality trait. On more occasions than I can count, people had pointed out to me that I was being my own worst enemy because of a particular course of conduct that I had chosen.

So, how was Belli his "own worst enemy?" How had he arrived at this place in the world that was described for me in that troubling newspaper article?

One huge disadvantage I had in trying to analyze the hows and whys of Belli's life at 88 was that our lives were unlike in so many ways He was known as the "King of Torts"—I am certain I will never have such a title. He had pioneered groundbreaking methodology for presenting evidence and witnesses in a trial setting. He had distinguished himself as the founder of the Association of American Trial Lawyers. He was founder and dean of the most prestigious trial lawyers' organization in America, the International Academy of Trial Lawyers. He had written 62 books on civil and criminal trial procedures. His list of clients read like *Who's Who in the World.*

The legend of Belli is a legend bigger than anything that I will ever be a part of. I am certain that I have read or been told on at least a dozen occasions that Belli, according to both his friends and his critics, was simply "bigger than life." More importantly, it was clear that Belli wanted to be "bigger than life."

Was there some relationship between Belli's wanting to be "bigger than life" and his being his own worst enemy?

There is a philosophical concept, probably first enunciated by the Gnostics, that can be summed up in the following equation: Grandiose expectations minus life's realities equal perpetual dissatisfaction with life. When we analyze that notion, it does not sound much different from the notion of "wanting to be bigger than life."

Paul Monzione was not only a law partner to Melvin Belli; he was also for many years his friend and protégé. He had this to say about him:

Belli was a paradox in that he possessed such tremendous compassion and understanding for the less fortunate people in our society, but didn't apply that keen understanding and genuine compassion to other parts of his life. Instead, he devoted a tremendous amount of energy to establishing, reestablishing, and maintaining the existence of his bigger-than-life image. He was a lawyer who could never really arrive because he never knew where he wanted to go. He simply wanted to go up: to be wealthy, more prestigious, more in control than anyone else he knew. I often had the impression that the best side of Belli's humanity was overshadowed by his destructive compulsion to be bigger than life. It was as if his 15 minutes of fame did not satisfy him. He needed to extend that 15 minutes to 30 minutes, then to an hour, then to an entire lifetime. "Belli" had to be a household word throughout the United

States for all time before he could ever find any sense of peace in his life.

The cost of the challenge of being bigger than real life is no less severe to many of us than it was Aesop's bullfrog. The routine of maintaining the image of being the biggest, most impressive bullfrog in our community most of the time weighs us down with some heavy baggage.

If we ever thoroughly rummage through that baggage, we are sure to find the following:

Big People Build Big Walls

First, always striving to be bigger than the biggest real-life creature in our pond separates us from almost all the other creatures. The lawyer wanting to be bigger than the real life around him will typically do a pretty good job detaching himself from the lives of family and friends.

About half the lawyers who responded to the survey in the appendix of this book said that they sometimes take the approval of their family for granted and pay too much attention to gaining the approval of their professional peers. Less than half the respondents were able to say that they devote enough energy to their personal relationships.

Trying to be bigger than life is sometimes easier than cultivating relationships with our family and friends. Our experience should tell us that ensuring the health of the really important relationships with our children, spouses, and closest friends usually will require authentic, focused, sometimes gut-wrenching effort on our part.

On the other hand, living with the goal of having our children, spouse, and friends constantly standing in awe of the "image" of what we are requires very little personal authenticity. It demands more showmanship than real substance in our relationships. Somewhere in the process of growing into our fantasy image of being the most impressive and powerful lawyer father, lawyer husband, and lawyer friend in our neighborhood, we talk ourselves into believing that that is what our family and friends want from us. Like any good showman, we begin tuning in to the sounds of applause. We focus more on the impersonal oohs and aahs from the crowd than on the faces of individuals in that crowd.

Diligent attention to good showmanship certainly moves us toward our goal of becoming bigger than life, but unfortunately it tends to separate us from important people.

The truth is that our family and friends are proud of our achievements. They usually recognize that our achievements frequently benefit them. But when that effort to overachieve becomes an unhealthy obsession, the important people in our lives begin to recognize the obvious: that our efforts to achieve usually benefit only one thing—our desire to be bigger than life.

There is a book in circulation that carries the title *Explaining the Inexplicable: The Rodent's Guide to Lawyers*. It was written by an immensely clever young lawyer who identifies him or herself as "The Rodent." The distilled substance of the book could be characterized as a brutal indictment of the culture that has developed within America's large law firms. The Rodent has an ability to transform the outrageous into insight about our profession's shortcomings. In the section "The Lawyer's Friends," The Rodent writes:

The only friends worth having are those who can advance the attorney's career. After the bar exam, friends of the lawyer's youth begin to drop off, having grown tired of repeated cancellations and attempts to solicit business by their former buddy. To fill the void, the lawyer finds new friends from major corporations who are in a position to refer legal work to The Firm.

As the lawyer becomes more senior, those ranking below her at The Firm will pretend to be her friends for their own selfish purposes. Even though they ridicule the lonesome attorney behind her back, these false friends offer the companionship and warmth lacking in the lawyer's life.

A partner's only real friends are other partners until, of course, the partner becomes an economic drain on The Firm. When this occurs, The Partner is forced out of The Firm and left friendless.

What is described in those few paragraphs is the result of professional myopia. It is a description of what the single-minded overachiever often leaves behind as he lives out his vision of becoming substantially bigger than everyone else.

The "Lawyer of the Year" and Her Uninvited Tagalongs

The next time you sit through one of those continuing legal education programs, take a few minutes and glance at the CV that is always included somewhere in the speaker's written material. I ran across one not long ago that covered two single-spaced typewritten pages. This speaker had been the highest-ranking officer in her state bar association. Her peers had declared that she was one of the most outstanding lawyers in her community. If my calculations were correct, there was a time when she was serving on 15 committees of one kind or another all at the same time. She had been president of this group or vice-president of that group almost from the time she got out of law school.

Nowhere in those two typewritten pages was there any mention of whether she was someone's wife or mother. It made me wonder: who was she doing all this for anyway? Reading between the lines of that CV, it was easy to recognize that wherever this "Lawyer of the Year" was going, she was distinguishing and separating herself from the overwhelming majority of average people she would probably come into contact with day to day. She was a lawyer who had devoted a huge portion of her 40-plus years to becoming the image of something that was distinctively bigger than the rest of the lawyer world around her.

But chances are that she had also been successful in separating herself from a good many people who did not demand, require, or even want her to grow into the shoes of the fantastic image she was trying to become. Her family and very closest friends would no doubt tell her that her unhealthy ego trip was a trip where they were uninvited tagalongs.

A Manageable Life is Not the Same as Mediocrity

Aesop was quick to praise effort and achievement. His fables praised hard work, imagination, and vision. It is usually the inventive, hardworking visionary that does well in Aesop's fables. It is always the unmotivated, shiftless loafer who not only does poorly for himself but also brings some degree of suffering to others who are counting on him. He used illustrations of foolish grasshoppers, lazy rabbits, and sluggish foxes to urge us to try to improve the quality of our lives. Nowhere in Aesop's fables is there a suggestion that the unmotivated quitter will live a happy life. His fables urge us to try to achieve. He was critical of our tendency to rationalize mediocrity.

One day a prideful fox noticed a ripe bunch of grapes hanging from a vine that had grown up the branches of a tree. The grapes appeared to be just out of the fox's reach. This fox loved the taste of ripe grapes, so he made a leap for the grapes, but they were too high. So he leaped again and almost reached them, but fell short. He tried to climb the tree a dozen times. He tried until he simply gave up. As he walked away, the fox told himself that he didn't really want those grapes. He rationalized that, although the grapes looked very tasty, they were probably sour, so it was probably just as well that he could not reach them.

Aesop's philosophy was that we should be vigilant in our effort to improve our lives. We should try to attain what might at first seem unattainable. But he also cautioned us that, as we try to achieve, there are a few traps we need to be aware of.

Odds and Expectations

Aesop's big bullfrog probably had another gremlin to deal with on a pretty regular basis. He probably was tormented by constantly living with unrealistic expectations about how big he should eventually become. Those gremlins no doubt caused him to use so much energy trying to be remembered for all time that he missed too much of the here and now.

Suppose you were to create a list of people whose names you believe will be remembered for all time. Create for yourself a mental list dating back to the very beginning of civilization—people who will more than likely always be remembered as long as there is a civilization still in place. What you would find is that the number of those special people as a percentage of the world population throughout history would be so small that it would be nearly impossible to express it in numeric form. Obviously, the odds are dramatically stacked against the individual who is living with the hope that civilization will remember him for all time.

The fatalist or pessimist might use those daunting odds to perpetuate an idea that we should learn to be forever satisfied with our place in life. But, this chapter is not about the virtues of fatalism. It has not been written to suggest that we accept our lot in life for what it is and stay floundering in that place for a lifetime. However, if we do choose to spend most of our 70-plus years on this earth trying to tower above real life, we at least need to have a notion about the odds of where we really will be at the end of that journey.

The odds are that, if we commit ourselves to it, we have the ability to make dramatic improvements in the way this world operates, but it is still unlikely that our contributions will cause us to be remembered for anything approaching "all time." When we can remain motivated toward real achievement, and at the same time avoid trampling on the best parts of our lives in hopes of being remembered forever, then we are living with the balance Aesop recommended.

Thousands of Forgotten Inventors Have Improved this World

Emerson begins one of his essays with this line: "It is natural to believe in great men." After that first line, Emerson devotes the rest of his essay to giving us a glimpse into what he believes are the limitations to that "greatness." Emerson points out that "Every carpenter who shaves with a foreplane borrows the genius of some forgotten inventor."

Perhaps the 1995 newspaper article that told of the sad demise of Mel Belli would have had a more peaceful, pleasant ending if Belli had understood that the generations of lawyers who would follow him would not expect him to have a name that would be remembered for all time. That newspaper article might have had a happier ending if Belli could ever have appreciated the tremendous honor that comes with simply growing into the shoes of just another "forgotten inventor."

Perhaps Belli could not get his arms around the idea that the overwhelming majority of the world's greatest achievers would probably be relegated to being merely "forgotten inventors." He never could appreciate the fact that, even though there would come a day when people had no idea who he was, those same people would have benefited from what he left behind. They would have benefited from his creativity, from his willingness to be a visionary and a risk taker.

Emerson analyzed the issue this way:

> Life is girt all round with a zodiac of sciences, the contributions of men who have perished to add their point of light to our sky. Engineer, broker, jurist, physician, moralist, theologian, and every man, inasmuch as he has

any science, is a definer and map-maker of the latitudes and longitudes of our condition. These road makers on every hand enrich us.

Aesop's frog was far less challenged in being the most impressive big frog in his pond until the day that damned bull showed up. The reality of "big" took on a whole new meaning around the pond that day. It would have been healthier for the big bullfrog to change his expectations about how big he realistically could become.

More than 77 percent of the lawyers whose thoughts are reflected in the appendix questionnaire believe that unrealistic career expectations rise to the level of being destructive for lawyers.

If that collective opinion is correct, then how are those expectations destructive? Rick Kuykendall started practicing law in 1981. These are his observations about unreasonable expectations:

Jerome "Buddy" Cooper graduated at the top of his class at Harvard Law School. He clerked for Justice Hugo Black from 1937 to

1940 and then returned to his home state of Alabama to become one of the most respected labor lawyers in America. Cooper always characterized his job as that of a servant, and he was a lion of a servant on behalf of the most powerless elements of our society. The fruits of that type of service are rarely financial. But Cooper sincerely never expected to grow rich practicing law. He was secure enough about who he was that he never wanted or expected to become a living legend. He never had to do better or have more than the other guy to be content about who he is.

I can honestly say that Cooper never had an ego that was so fragile that he had to rely on attention and accolades to calibrate his self-worth. He became a lawyer so that he could serve people. Tom Brokaw described the Buddy Coopers of this world in a book entitled *The Greatest Generation.*

On most days practicing law, I cannot find any more Buddy Coopers in the crowd of lawyers that are my contemporaries. Instead, it is much easier to identify lawyers who are rarely content with where they stand in their careers. Their expectations for greater and greater financial success has practically obliterated their commitment to service. I am fearful that our profession has lost the spirit and commitment of lawyers like Buddy Cooper. Our unreasonable expectations have turned us into legal entrepreneurs. We have focused on achievement to the point that our expectations have become not only unreasonable, but unhealthy on both a personal and professional level. Those unhealthy expectations have done harm to our commitment to service.

Aesop's bullfrog lived in a small pond community. On most days, his challenge to be bigger than the other inhabitants of that community was not terribly difficult. Our lawyering world is much different. Our expectations do not have us competing simply with lawyers down the street. We will need to puff up big enough to compete with lawyers from the East Coast to the West Coast. Our expectations about how big we can become are gauged against the lives of a large group of over achievers.

The next time you go to one of those annual lawyer conventions, take notice of those lawyers walking around with red, blue, gold, and white ribbons pinned to their chests. Occasionally, you will see them wearing impressive-looking name badges that give you not only their name but almost a thumbnail review of their devotion to accomplishment. Realize that they are lawyers who probably are perceived by other lawyers as having a national reputation exceeding yours. They probably have received honors or accolades for the way they have distinguished themselves in their endless effort to achieve. Chances are many of them are making substantially more money than you. At the end of their careers, many of them will have at least a few of those timeless special achievement awards. During that convention, they will move comfortably through circles of lawyers who are regarded as leaders within this profession, circles that you may not feel a part of.

Now, take a moment for a reality check, and ask yourself: *Am I comfortable with that?* Are your expectations for yourself as a lawyer such that you do not feel disappointment, resentment, disillusionment, jealousy, or anger over the fact that you are not a member of that close circle of overachievers? If your reality check does not uncover a host of negative emotions, that may indicate that you do not have your professional expectations leveraged to unhealthy levels. Perhaps you are truthfully able to say that you are today living in accordance with your expectations.

Unfortunately, there are too many lawyers in our ranks who would not fare so well with such a reality check. They are lawyers who can never feel peaceful about *this* reality:

Someone, somewhere today is out-achieving them. Someone is acquiring a bigger fortune. Someone is living a life tremendously more glamorous, more comfortable, possibly more rewarding. Someone will always have more and be more no matter how much of our lives we waste raising unhealthy expectations about how big we will someday become.

Aesop used a gnat and a cow to illustrate the point:

One day, a gnat was flying over the head of a cow making as much noise as he possibly could to attract the cow's attention. The gnat landed on one of the cow's horns, believing that surely the cow would take notice of him. After sitting on the cow's horn for a while, the gnat was preparing to move on to a place where he would draw more attention. Before he left, however, he said to the cow; "I guess you are pleased to see me leave." The cow's answer must have been a great disappointment to the gnat: "I was not even aware that you were here."

Maintaining unrealistic images about ourselves can be exhausting. Forty-seven percent of the respondents to the questionnaire said that no matter how much money they make, they are always working to make more. Eighty-nine percent said that they believe lawyers' spending beyond their financial ability is a behavior that is destructive within our profession.

Those types of descriptions by lawyers of lawyers conjure up an image similar to the poor old bullfrog puffing himself up bigger and bigger to impress the smaller denizens of his pond.

When we can learn to accept what the gnat was unable to accept, we will be able to better control our need to raise one unreasonable expectation after another as we move from accomplishment to accomplishment in order to maintain an enhanced reality about ourselves. It might even become possible to convince ourselves that it is actually unhealthy to feel that no matter how much money we make, we should always try to make more.

Growing Bigger Than Life's
Small and Simple Pleasures

Forever trying to be bigger than real life not only separates us from people, it often separates us from parts of everyday living that could be more rewarding to us if we would only allow for it.

In the questionnaire used as the foundation for my book *In Search of Atticus Finch,* a few of the questions were designed to find out to what extent lawyers were cultivating interests outside their law offices. For example, one question asked how many non-law courses they had enrolled in at their local college or university since they graduated from law school. Less than 15 percent had ever enrolled in even one course. Most lawyers will candidly admit that they have a business to run, and any activity that does not easily blend with running that business takes a position of extremely low priority.

For example, it becomes difficult to place much importance in the intrinsic value of educating ourselves if we do not see a relationship between that education and dividends. Most lawyers who are helplessly caught up in legal empire building would never see much value in enrolling in a philosophy or humanities course just for the sake of learning something new. They cannot get past their lifetime of training themselves to pay attention mostly—sometimes exclusively—to efforts that pay dividends of some kind. Aesop explained it this way:

A proud rooster was scratching around in the dirt looking for chicken feed. In the process, he uncovered a huge emerald. The rooster scarcely paid attention to the beauty of the emerald. He left it on the ground, hardly giving it a second glance, and continued scratching around in the dirt. The emerald had no value to the rooster. It was food he was after.

In order to make a living as a lawyer, we will be required to do a fair amount of scratching around in the dirt as we hunt for food. Too often, however, we become caught up in building empires…in creating a name and image for ourselves that will in our minds be remembered for all time. On our way to building a name and reputation that we believe will be timeless, we leave far too many emeralds lying in the dirt unnoticed.

Sam Viviano practiced law for 30 years. During those years, he learned to place importance and value on parts of living that did not pay money dividends.

There came a time in my years practicing law that I realized I was hiring people to help carry out almost every task of my day-to-day living. I paid for people to cook. I paid for handymen to make the most simple repairs around my house. I hired gardeners to take care of our flower gardens. I hired people to take care of the teakwood on my boats. People were even polishing and servicing cars that I had bought as hobby cars. When I owned a fish tank, I would even hire professionals to take care of the fish that lived in that tank.

I had managed to thoroughly disconnect from what some people might call the "chores" of day-to-day living. I had become so absorbed with being a successful lawyer that no part of my imagination or manpower was focused on anything that did not help keep my office doors open.

One weekend I did the unthinkable. My wife convinced me that I might actually enjoy doing some manual labor in a new rose garden she was planting behind our home. I reminded her that I paid the gardener to plant roses. But she persisted and made it sound like a new adventure that I would be foolish to pass up.

Five years later, I was still digging, planting, cutting, grafting, and thoroughly enjoying the rewards that that garden offered me every morning I worked in it.

I never made a single dollar working in that rose garden.

Chapter Eight
Becoming

THERE ONCE WAS A TINY TADPOLE *that lived in a very small pond. Around that pond lived many of the tadpole's friends: a few dragonflies, some earthworms, and several butterflies. The friendship the tiny tadpole had developed with the other inhabitants of that pond was important to him.*

As time passed, however, the tadpole began worrying that his friends were becoming more scarce.

There were no longer as many dragonflies, butterflies, and earthworms living around the pond. Not only were his friends disappearing, he also noticed that his remaining friends were not willing to spend much time around him. He had a notion that they were avoiding him. In fact, at one point, he actually began to believe that they were afraid of him.

One day he found himself sitting alone on the edge of that pond. He sensed that something was different about his life. A dragonfly buzzing overhead broke the news to him that it was not the pond that had changed. "Look at yourself in the water," he suggested.

Doing as the dragonfly advised, he saw in the pond the reflection of a very odd-looking creature. The dragonfly explained that he had changed from tadpole to toad so gradually that he had not noticed that he now had four legs. The dragonfly told the perplexed former tadpole that his home was now above the water, not below, and that the other creatures he had once called friends were now his food.

At that instant, the huge toad instinctively, as if unaware of what he was doing, stretched out his long toad tongue and pulled the dragonfly out of the air. He then hopped farther around the edge of the pond to discover what else was different about his life.

It is tough to be critical of the toad because he was, after all, destined to be a toad from the moment he came into the world as a tadpole. Fortunately, unlike the toad, we should have some control over what we are becoming every day. But in order to have control over the evolution of our character, doesn't it make sense that we should have a vision of what we want the end product to be? Doesn't it seem appropriate to then spend a substantial part of our time and energy trying to get there?

Shouldn't some small part of our 10-to-12–hour working day be devoted to labors, exercises, sacrifices, studies, maybe even ceremonies that help us develop and incorporate into our character those authentic foundations that Aesop believed improve our lives?

In the course of living those 10-to-12–hour days that are filled mostly with our Herculean efforts to help our material world evolve, shouldn't we reserve some energy for ensuring that our character is evolving as well?

Aesop's lifetime work of reducing his philosophy to two- and three-paragraph stories about everything from giving to greed could accurately be referred to as "reminders." They probably were not written with the purpose of mapping brand-new roads for character building. Rather, they were written as reminders to stop, look, listen, move forward, yield, and maybe even detour as our character becomes more matured, more of age.

Aesop's parables were obviously not written for people who had abandoned the belief that throughout our lifetime we should transform our character to something better. Instead, it is fairly clear that his fables were directed toward people who already attached some importance to the belief that they should actively help their character evolve.

Postmodern psychologists have been successful in creating labels for the various stages of character development that we should predictably move through in our lifetimes. They tell us that there are some stages of character development that are generally common to the human species. As our character develops, our id confronts our ego. Our ego should complement our superego. Our emotional balance, our character equilibrium, our spiritual symmetry are all dependent on these character parts developing properly, with one stage of progressive development yielding to the next in a way that results in something that looks like character maturity.

There are parts of our character makeup that need the same kind of exercise and attention we give to ourselves at the gym when we are trying to improve the quality of our ever-maturing bodies.

We want to help those bodies through the inevitable transitions that they must make as they age. We are forever trying to add a little muscle mass here, shave a few pounds there, increase physical stamina, and maybe turn a few heads with our physical appearance. We have some specific places and times that we put our bodies through set routines to accomplish all that.

According to thinkers and philosophers such as Aesop, there are some character qualities that also function better with a little exercise and attention.

For example, self-obsessed arrogance does not need much exercise in order to develop within our character, but unselfish humility does require quite a lot of attention and exercise if we are going to make it part of a day-to-day personal achievement. The tendency to extract for ourselves as much as we can from every person, situation, opportunity, or advantage that we happen upon comes naturally for many of us. But to give back when we don't have to, to give back more than we take, to replace greed with a spirit of giving requires a phenomenal amount of attention and exercise.

The same comparisons can appropriately be made when we develop a goal of strengthening our character by replacing a tendency toward dishonesty with honesty or cowardice with courage. Those same comparisons can be made when we are training ourselves to be a bit kinder and more compassionate in a lawyers' world that seems to pay tribute to "power with attitude" regardless of how that power with attitude affects people's lives.

We have to build our character the same way we build our material world, the same way we improve the quality of our physical appearance. We have to be willing to work at it.

Writings such as Aesop's fables don't arm us with new and special techniques. We don't need Aesop's fables to tell us how to give, how to show compassion, how to incorporate some constructive humility in our lives. But we might need to be reminded from time to time what our instincts are telling us: that such things actually improve our lives.

The writer Azizah al-Hibri is a legal scholar who was for many years a corporate lawyer on Wall Street. In 1996, in an article that appeared in the *Texas Tech Law Review*, she wrote:

> Working on Wall Street, it was "business" eighteen to twenty-four hours a day. It was the height of market activity, and law firms were leveraging their human resources to the hilt. Driven by the Qur'anic injunction to do my job well, I put in long hours. But my firm and I were not quite on the same page. The firm wanted to maximize its profits, while offering quality services. I wanted to oblige. Yet I was hampered in my efforts by my ambivalence about the system.

There was no time to perform my five daily prayers, even in a corner of my office. It was not possible to fast the month of Ramadan or even celebrate my holidays. How could I when I had to work and bill every working moment of my long days and nights?

Azizah al-Hibri devotes the better part of her article to showing lawyers how the observance of Ramadan and the ceremony of five daily prayers allowed her to remember that her life as a Wall Street corporate lawyer was inextricably connected to her life outside her office. She tells us that "you cannot, for example, decide to be dishonest in the office and be a good Muslim, Christian, or Jew at home." She tells us that, as lawyers, we will improve our lives and the lives of people we serve when we begin to understand that there are some authentic truths, some moral rules that are supposed to permeate every aspect of our lives.

For al-Hibri, the time she sets aside for remembering those authentic truths is during her five daily prayers, when her head is bowed toward Mecca. That is a time when she engages in reality checks that help her take an inventory of how her character development is coming along day to day. She has not allowed herself to become hopelessly unsophisticated or naïvely artless with regard to her character. It is at those five times a day that she is exercising a few character qualities that will help improve her life and the lives of people she serves.

Unlike the tadpole that has made the unavoidable, inevitable transition to a full-grown toad, al-Hibri recognizes that she has been blessed with the ability to *influence* what she is evolving into day by day.

Appendix
The Survey Results

I sometimes find that I defer enjoying life while I work toward arriving at a consistent level of income that I can feel comfortable with.

    72%   Yes

    28%   No

I have enough of everything right now to relax and feel content.

    32%   Yes

    68%   No

Before I can say that I am truly "financially secure," I will have to feel that I am "financially secure" for the next:

    18%   5 years

    13%   12 years

    36%   20 years

    33%   I don't know if I will ever feel financially secure enough.

I sometimes feel that my efforts to maintain financial security cause me:

- 20% Fear
- 49% Anxiety
- 14% No negative emotions at all
- 17% To become more self-centered

The following statement(s) describe(s) my attitude about power and prestige as a lawyer *(check all that apply):*

- 57% Attaining power and prestige is at least a moderately important goal to me.
- 54% I feel that I have already attained a completely satisfactory level of power and prestige as a lawyer.
- 36% Arriving at a high level of power and prestige as a lawyer is simply unimportant to me.
- 66% I believe most lawyers place too much emphasis on attaining power and prestige.
- 48% I often get tired of the struggle for power and prestige.

I am at the point in my career where I have accumulated enough financial wealth to allow me to fully enjoy life.

- 24% Yes
- 76% No

I find myself judging my success as a lawyer according to the amount of financial success I am able to achieve.

- 45% Yes
- 55% No

If I could manage to consistently average the following income per year, I would be completely content and at ease with my role as a lawyer:

40%	$150,000
32%	$300,000
20%	$500,000
4%	$750,000
1%	$1 million
3%	More than $1 million

The following statement(s) describe(s) my attitudes about ego *(check all that apply):*

71%	I believe I have a completely healthy ego.
40%	I wish I had the ability to better control and direct my ego.
30%	I have become more self-centered since I began practicing law.
52%	I would characterize most lawyers I know as being overly self-centered.
16%	A grandiose ego is actually a positive trait in the world of complex litigation these days.
76%	I believe many of my fellow attorneys have allowed their unhealthy ego to do damage to our profession.

Images that are sold to me by the media (e.g., magazines, TV, movies) have the following effect(s) on my lifestyle:

24%	I have never considered the possible impact they have on me.
30%	They push me toward greater achievement.
59%	I always recognize that they are illusory.
46%	I feel those images push me toward being more materialistic than I would prefer.
60%	I regard "trendy" people as being weak and impressionable.

I have known people in the lawyering profession whose ambition I would consider equivalent to an *addiction*.

88%   Yes

12%   No

I believe that ambition within our profession does have the potential to take on an addictive nature.

97%   Yes

3%   No

The following is/are true of me *(check all that apply):*

27%   As soon as I reach most of my financial and personal goals, I will devote more energy to becoming a kinder, gentler person.

50%   I already devote more than enough energy to my personal relationships even though I have not reached most of my financial and personal goals.

45%   I sometimes take the approval of my family for granted and pay too much attention to gaining approval from my professional peers.

Would you characterize yourself as having a tendency to raise your expectations a little bit higher each time you rise to another level of accomplishment?

88%   Yes

12%   No

Do you now work harder than you really want to?

61%   Yes

39%   No

Do you worry about your future financial success?

77%   Yes

23%   No

The following statement(s) describe(s) my attitude *(check all that apply):*

47%	No matter how much money I make, I am always working to make more.
50%	I am a member of at least one organization not because I enjoy it but because it is good for my career.
60%	My professional peers worry about financial success far more than I do.
21%	I could stop working today and make ends meet financially for myself and my family.
67%	The more successful I appear to be, the more business I will get as a lawyer.

I have observed the following behaviors rise to the level of being destructive within my profession as a lawyer:

82%	Substance abuse
92%	Overworking
77%	Unrealistic career expectations
89%	Overspending beyond financial ability
92%	Pushing the limits of acceptable ethical conduct
97%	Accepting more work than can feasibly be accomplished

If I had been born independently wealthy, I could most likely have felt peaceful and content being a(n) *(choose two):*

25%	Writer
22%	College professor
12%	Full-time philanthropist
11%	Politician
7%	Explorer
6%	Spiritual leader of some kind
5%	Entertainer

4%   Horticulturist

3%   Diving instructor

2%   Ski instructor

2%   Airplane pilot

Every year my financial obligations are:

52%   Increasing

16%   Decreasing

32%   Remaining the same

I give to charity:

17%   More than 1% of my income

34%   More than 5% of my income

17%   More than 10% of my income

32%   No set percentage

I find myself feeling guilty about not giving enough to charitable causes.

40%   Yes

60%   No

The following statement(s) is/are true of me *(check all that apply):*

89%   I would dislike being considered "average" by my peers.

79%   I enjoy being in a position of authority.

48%   I feel that what I do for a living is significantly more important than what most other people do for a living.

47%   Luck has played a very insignificant role in my level of success.

My rating in Martindale-Hubbell is:

50%	AV
24%	BV
13%	CV
13%	Other

And that rating is very important to me.

39%	Yes
61%	No

Throughout my years of lawyering I have given very little thought to the concepts covered in this questionnaire.

26%	Yes
74%	No